D0069596

HEROES OF HISTORY

WILLIAM PENN

Liberty and Justice for All

HEROES OF HISTORY

WILLIAM PENN

Liberty and Justice for All

JANET & GEOFF BENGE

Emerald
Books

P.O. BOX 635, LYNNWOOD, WA 98046

Emerald Books are distributed through YWAM Publishing. For a full list of titles, including other great biographies, visit our website at www.ywampublishing.com or call 1-800-922-2143.

Library of Congress Cataloging-in-Publication Data

Benge, Janet, 1958–
    William Penn : liberty and justice for all / Janet and Geoff Benge.
        p. cm. — (Heroes of history)
Includes bibliographical references.
Summary: A biography of William Penn, the founder of Pennsylvania and a Quaker advocate for justice and religious tolerance in Great Britain and the American colonies.
    ISBN 1-883002-82-6
  1. Penn, William, 1644–1718—Juvenile literature.
2. Pioneers—Pennsylvania—Biography—Juvenile literature.
3. Quakers—Pennsylvania—Biography—Juvenile literature.
4. Pennsylvania—History—Colonial period, ca. 1600-1775—Juvenile literature. [1. Penn, William, 1644-1718. 2. Pioneers. 3. Quakers.
4. Pennsylvania—History—Colonial period, ca. 1600–1775.] I. Benge, Geoff, 1954– II. Title.
    F152.2 .B46 2002
    974.8'02'092—dc21

                                          2001007283

William Penn: Liberty and Justice for All
Copyright © 2002 by Janet and Geoff Benge

10 09 08 07 06 05 04   10 9 8 7 6 5 4 3 2

Published by Emerald Books
P.O. Box 635
Lynnwood, Washington 98046

ISBN 1-883002-82-6

Printed in the United States of America.

HEROES OF HISTORY

Biographies

John Adams
Clara Barton
Daniel Boone
George Washington Carver
Christopher Columbus
Benjamin Franklin
Meriwether Lewis
Abraham Lincoln
Douglas MacArthur
William Penn
Theodore Roosevelt
Harriet Tubman
George Washington

More Heroes of History coming soon!
Unit study curriculum guides are available
for select biographies.

Available at your local bookstore or
through Emerald Books
1 (800) 922-2143

In memory of Professor J. Ivon Graham,
1888–1983
A true Quaker and a special friend

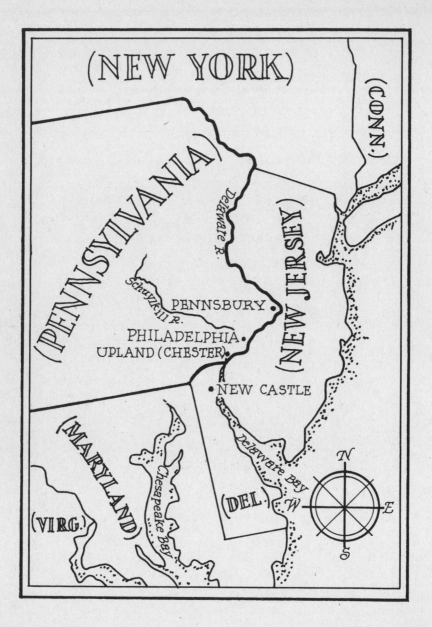

Contents

Chapter 1

My Prison Shall Be My Grave

U p you go," a guard said as he shoved William Penn toward the worn stone staircase that twisted its way to the top of the large square tower.

As William stumbled forward, he caught a glimpse of one of the old torture chambers with the rack still inside. The rack was a crude mechanical device that had been used to get inmates to confess. The prisoner was tied to the device and suffered in agony as notch by notch the wheel was turned and the person's body was stretched. When the pain became too unbearable, most prisoners confessed to a crime, whether or not they had committed one. Those who refused to confess were stretched until their bones dislocated and their flesh pulled apart. William felt a shiver run up his spine as he walked past the chamber.

As a young boy William had often played within the shadow of the infamous Tower of London. Sometimes he had watched as prisoners were marched inside or he had heard bloodcurdling screams come from deep within the prison. But he had never for a moment imagined being one of those locked up in this place. How could he have? He was the son of Sir William Penn, one of the most famous men in England, an admiral in the Royal Navy and a confidant to the king. William had enjoyed a rich and privileged life, and now he was to be locked up in the Tower of London. He could scarcely believe it.

Several rats scurried away in front of him as the two men approached the top of the tower. William had to stoop to enter the small cell at the head of the stairs.

"See how you like this, then," the soldier mocked. "From what I hear, there's no fancy visitors for you and none of those books you're so fond of quoting, either."

A heavy oak door with a barred opening in it slammed shut behind William. He stumbled to the middle of the room and stretched out his arms. He could touch all four of the cold, slimy walls. A barred window let in a shaft of hazy light that illuminated a bucket and a pile of straw, the only items in the room. William spread the straw out on the floor and lay down.

As he lay there, William wondered what would happen next. Surely he would not be locked up forever without someone protesting on his behalf.

Finally, after several days alone in his cell, the bishop of London sent William a message that read, "Recant in Common Garden at an appointed time before all the City, or else be a prisoner for life."

So that was it. All he had to do was say he did not mean what he had written and he would be free to leave the tower. It was quite an offer. At an earlier time he might have jumped at it, but not now. He meant what he wrote, and he was prepared to spend the rest of his life in prison defending his words if that is what it took. Defending liberty and justice was more important to William than being a free man at the cost of compromising his conscience.

William wrote back to the bishop, "Thou mayst tell my father, whom I know will ask thee, these words, that my prison shall be my grave before I will budge a jot, for I owe my conscience to no mortal man. I have no need to fear. God will make amends for all." If William had to spend the rest of his life in this cold, dank, rat-infested prison, then so be it.

As William sat in the corner contemplating his bleak future, his mind wandered back to happier times during his childhood in Wanstead....

Chapter 2

A National Hero

Four-year-old William Penn walked carefully up the steps to his house. Cupped in his hands was a bird's nest he had found in the hedge. It was midwinter, and the nests that once were hidden by green foliage and filled with baby robins were now clearly visible and empty.

Setting the nest down, William took off his coat before running to show his mother his latest treasure. He was just approaching her chamber when he heard an unfamiliar sound. Behind the closed door someone, an adult, was sobbing. William cracked the door and peered inside. His mother was sitting on the bed, her head in her hands. Beside her was one of their neighbors.

"I thought you'd like to know as soon as I heard from London," the woman was saying to Mrs. Penn.

William watched as his mother lifted her head and forced a smile.

"Of course. But what a thing to do! Who can believe it? The Roundheads have chopped off the king's head! There's never been a day like this in all of history. To think of people rising up against the man God placed over us and killing him. What will happen now? Poor King Charles," she wailed.

After gently shutting the door, William crept away to his own room. As he sat on his bed, the bird's nest forgotten, he tried to work out what he had just heard. He had seldom seen his mother cry before, and even then it was just a tear or two when his father, Captain William Penn, Sr., went back to sea. *The king's death must be a very sad thing,* William thought to himself.

William didn't know a lot about the king, though he had heard his father talk about him and once he'd seen a painting of the king holding two huge falcons. "Your grandfather, Giles Penn, gave those birds to His Majesty," William's father had told him. "He was a sea captain like me, and if he found something he thought the king would like on one of his voyages, he'd bring it back for him. They were friends, you know."

Several days later, as he sat at the table eating rabbit pie, William asked, "Mama, if the old king is dead, who is the new king?"

Mrs. Penn looked at William for a long time and then drew a deep breath. "There won't be a new a king. We have a parliament and a commonwealth now, and Oliver Cromwell is their leader," she said.

Indeed, deep political changes had taken place in England, but it would be several more years before William fully understood the impact of what had happened that cold January day in 1649 when King Charles was executed.

Even though the king was gone, not a lot changed in William's small world—a house and farm located in Wanstead, Essex, eleven miles northeast of the wall that surrounded the city of London. However, big changes took place in other parts of Great Britain. The country had been in turmoil for years. King Charles had been authoritarian in his rule, levying high taxes on the people of Britain to pay for his extravagant lifestyle. As well, for eleven years he refused to convene Parliament. When finally, under pressure, he called Parliament back together, the Puritan-dominated assembly decided it was time for change. The power of the autocratic king had to be curtailed, they argued. England needed to become a more open place, where the religious freedoms of others were respected. To help achieve this end, Cromwell, a brilliant general, raised and trained a people's army that became known as the New Model Army. After several decisive victories, Cromwell and his army finally won the day. King Charles fled England to Scotland, but the Scots sold him back to the English, and he was beheaded upon his return.

With the king gone, Cromwell and those members of Parliament loyal to Puritan ideals set about refashioning English society. In keeping with their notion of religious freedom, they allowed Jews to return to Britain after 350 years of being banished from the country. And strict observance of the Sabbath was put in place. No work was to be done on Sunday, the day for attending church and engaging in religious reflection.

Although Cromwell wanted greater religious freedom and tolerance, he soon began a campaign to stamp out those religious views he did not like. His first target was Ireland, where the pope had declared that it was permitted for Catholics to wage war on their Protestant neighbors. Cromwell was determined to make the Irish submit to his Protestant parliament. His plan was ruthless and simple. Any Irish Catholics who would not convert to the Church of England were either driven off their land or killed. Also, twelve thousand Irish Catholics were sold as slaves in the West Indies, where, no doubt, many of them often wished they had been killed in their homeland instead.

William knew that his mother had lived in Ireland with her first husband, a Dutch trader. After a year of marriage her husband had died, leaving William's mother a widow. Soon afterward Irish Catholics attacked the Dutch and English in their colony at Kilrush, on the Shannon River, and William's mother had had to flee to England with little more than the clothes on her back. She seldom talked about the ordeal, and William thought she must be happy now that the Irish were getting a whipping from Oliver Cromwell.

Before long, when William Penn was six, Cromwell and the Roundheads, as Puritan supporters were called, marched into Scotland. It was there that King Charles's son, also called Charles, was trying to mount an attack on England to reclaim his father's crown. The Prince of Wales, as the young Charles was known, barely escaped Scotland with his life. He quickly fled to Europe.

On the heels of the skirmish with Scotland came war with the Netherlands. William's father, who had now been promoted to admiral, was home less than ever.

Still, William had plenty to keep him busy. He now had a baby sister named Margaret, whom he liked to carry around. He was also attending Chigwell School, where the hours were long and tiring for him, though he found the schoolwork easy and could memorize just about anything he set his mind to. School started in the dark at six in the morning with catechism and prayers. Then came lessons in Greek and English literature. The boys stopped for lunch at eleven o'clock, and then it was back to classes at one for English grammar, Latin, spelling, and moral training. One of the things William enjoyed most about getting to and from school was running. He loved to run like the wind, and he could cover the three miles between home and school without stopping.

The only problem with running was that William had to hold his wig in place. It would have embarrassed him greatly if it flew off while he ran and his fellow students saw his bald head. When he was three, William contracted smallpox, and the illness had left him permanently bald. His mother told him he should be grateful. Most children did not survive smallpox, and those who did usually had hideously scarred faces. Compared to that, she told him, a bald head was easy to bear, though William did not always feel so grateful.

The ability to run fast came in handy the day one of the house servants came to fetch William from school. "Hurry home, lad, your mother has the coach ready!" the servant said. And that's just what William did. As he sprinted down the lanes flanked with hedgerows, he wondered what could possibly be so important that his mother had sent for him.

An hour later William was sitting in the family coach, dressed in his best clothes and on his way to London to see his father's arrival from the Battle of Texel. As they wound their way along, William looked out the coach window at the narrow, dirty, overcrowded streets of London. On the banks of the River Thames, a large crowd had gathered in the late summer sun. Mrs. Penn and William joined the crowd and waited patiently. Soon their patience was rewarded. Around a bend in the river came the *James*, the flagship of the British Third Fleet, commanded by William's father. The ship bobbed large and proud in the river, square sails billowing from her three masts. Soon William could make out the fine detail of the ship's carved poop deck. Thirty-five cannons protruded proud and victorious from each side of the ship. William could also make out signs of the fierce battle the ship had been through. A number of her hull timbers were shattered from the impact of Dutch cannonballs. Even so, it was all a magnificent sight, one nine-year-old William Penn would never forget.

The next evening, back at the family home in Wanstead, William's father invited several friends to dinner. There, over tankards of beer, platters of sausage, and roast lamb, the details of the battle came rolling out. William listened intently from his perch by the fire.

"Insulted us they did," William's father said, banging the table with his fist. "Van Tromp hung a broom from his main mast as a sign of how the Dutch were going to sweep us off the ocean. That was his mistake. I've never seen the men so incensed. They were determined to teach the Dutch a lesson."

Admiral Penn took a large gulp of beer before continuing. "We fought our way through thirty escort ships before we trained our cannons on van Tromp's ship. When we were done, his ship's masts were broken and the broom was dragging in the water. But we weren't done with him yet. We moved in closer and with our grappling hooks pulled ourselves alongside and boarded his ship. You should have seen the look on van Tromp's face: absolute disbelief that this could be happening to him. And still we weren't done with him. We forced him and his crew below the deck of their ship and blew them up with their own gunpowder."

The men around the table raised their silver tankards in a victory salute.

"The Dutch won't be bothering us again," William's father said triumphantly.

"I hear Cromwell has rewarded you well," one of the guests said, staring at the gold chain around the admiral's neck.

"Yes," William's father replied, stroking it, "a gift from Oliver Cromwell. And I have been made 'General of the Sea.' Imagine that, Cromwell creating a new rank just for me."

The men around the table looked approvingly at one another.

William's father was given something else that was much more valuable than the gold chain or promotion in rank. It was land, lots of land, in Ireland. Cromwell was still trying to get Irish Catholics to give up both their faith and their language, but they were very stubborn. His new plan involved confiscating Irish land and giving it to Englishmen he wanted to honor. This served two purposes. First, Cromwell was able to reward men like Admiral Penn for their bravery on behalf of the Commonwealth, and second, it was an effective way to break up Irish society.

William did not think about who owned the land before his father was given it. He was filled with boyish fantasies now that his family had its own Irish castle at Macroom, about twenty miles west of Cork. However, it did not look as though William would get to see the castle anytime soon. His father was a rising star in Cromwell's master plan to make Great Britain the ruler of the seas.

At school, where William was always near the top of his class, many of his friends asked about his father. "What's it like having such a hero for a father?" and "Do you want to go to sea and be an admiral, too?"

William wasn't sure how to answer the second question. He knew his own father had gone to sea at ten years of age and had been the captain of his own ship plying the Mediterranean coast by the time he was seventeen. But the sea did not beckon William. He would never have told his father this, but he preferred roaming in the woods that surrounded their house over heading out to sea in a ship.

It was not long before Admiral Penn was off again. This time he was going much farther afield than Europe. Now that the war with Holland was over, Cromwell had decided to pick a fight with the Spanish. It was time, he announced, for Great Britain to make its presence felt in the New World. Spain had had its way in the West Indies for too long. Now none other than Admiral Penn, General of the Sea, was going to lead a glorious fleet carrying army General Robert Venables and seven thousand troops to Hispaniola and take the island for the British. From that foothold, they would launch an attack on Spanish settlements in America.

Since about 1500 all of the farmable land in Europe had been used up; there were no more frontiers to break in. As a result both England and Spain wanted what America had plenty of—land. So Admiral Penn sailed amidst much fanfare on Christmas Day, 1654, to the edge of the new frontier—America.

In many ways William was glad his father had left again. He could not explain it to his school friends, but it was not easy living with a national hero. His father had been at sea nearly all of his life, and he was used to giving orders, something that he continued to do at home. Admiral Penn rarely talked to his son, or his wife for that matter, except to bark out a command. William noticed that everyone, even the cook and the coachman, looked happier when his father was off fighting.

In September of the following year, just after William had returned to school, a servant once again summoned him from class. This time, though, it was not to bask in his father's latest victory.

"What is wrong, Mama?" William asked when he saw his mother's grim face.

"We have to go to London now. I am going to leave your sister Peggy with her nurse." She hesitated for a moment. "You are nearly eleven now, and you will find out soon enough for yourself. Something has gone terribly wrong. Your father is imprisoned in the Tower of London!"

William stood there trying to grasp the information. Every time his father came back from a voyage, he was given a new title and many other rewards. What could possibly have gone so wrong this time?

As it turned out, a lot had gone wrong. Admiral Penn had played his part well. He had delivered General Venables and his troops to Hispaniola. But the general had not expected the kind of war he quickly became engaged in. No one, it seemed, had given the natives on the island the textbook on fighting a respectable European war. Instead of lining up for staged battles, the natives crept through the forest and shot arrows at the unfortunate British soldiers. When the British wheeled around to face them, they were gone, leaving flashes of brown among the trees. Unable to gain access to any of the rivers or streams on the island, the British ran out of drinking water. It was hot, hotter than they had ever experienced before, and soon the soldiers retreated to the ships, too exhausted and disheartened to try to take the island again.

General Venables, seeing it was hopeless to press his men to fight on the steamy, mountainous island anymore, had made a decision to head for Jamaica instead. Surely, he told Admiral Penn, that would be much easier to capture and just as good a jewel to claim for the Commonwealth.

Jamaica proved much easier to subdue, and soon the fleet was headed home, the British flag flying proudly over the new Jamaican colony. However, Cromwell was not impressed. When he said capture Hispaniola, he meant *capture Hispaniola!* As a result Admiral Penn and General Venables were both thrown into the Tower of London as soon as they returned.

As William sat in the coach with his mother, he wondered what would happen next. Would his father be beheaded as the king had been? Would that make William the new "man" of the family?

Chapter 3

A Simple Message

Time dragged on as William and his mother waited for Admiral Penn's case to come to trial. The holdup in the case occurred because Cromwell would not actually charge William's father with anything. There were rumors that the Lord Protector, the title by which Cromwell now called himself, was holding Admiral Penn while he gathered evidence of his treason in not staying and capturing Hispaniola as he had been instructed to do. But as time went by, the public began to ask why their hero was in prison. Eventually, after five weeks in jail, Admiral Penn was offered his freedom on two conditions: that he publicly apologize to Cromwell for disobeying him and that he not go back to sea.

The apology was made, and the family returned to their home in Wanstead. Now, for the first time since he was ten years old, William's father was stuck on land. He tried to make the most of it, but it was not easy for him supervising the planting of crops on the estate and collecting the rent from peasant farmers. Nor was it easy to live in Puritan England. Cromwell seemed to make up more and more rules to stop everyone from having fun. By now all of the theaters, art exhibits, running races, and bowling competitions had been shut down. Even cockfighting and card playing were things of the past, and bright clothing and laughter were frowned upon. And nothing, it seemed, was fit to do on Sunday except go to church three times and read the Bible. Inns and taverns were also closed for the Sabbath, making it difficult for travelers to go any distance.

"As soon as the baby's born, we are leaving England," William's father told him one day as they were riding around the estate together.

"Really?" William replied, his heart racing. "Where are we going?"

"Ireland," his father answered. "Oliver Cromwell's rule cannot last forever, and I think the best thing to do is to lie low until it's over. Then we will come back to England and help rebuild the country. Mind you, don't breathe a word of what I've told you to anyone, or I could end up back in the Tower of London."

William gulped. "No, Father," he replied. "Will I be able to go to school in Ireland?"

The admiral shook his head. "There's no suitable school for a son of mine in that backward place," he said, flicking the reins of his horse. "I have your schoolmaster looking for a tutor to take with us."

They rode on in silence as William tried to think through all the implications of this new knowledge. As far as he knew, his mother was due to have the baby in early summer. That meant they would probably be aboard a ship for Ireland by August! Finally he was going to see the castle and have some adventures of his own.

The baby arrived in due course and was named Richard. William thought he was a cute little thing with fuzzy brown hair, while his four-year-old sister, Margaret, wanted to hold him and poke him at the same time.

Now that William was nearly twelve years old, he noticed that the family often split in two. His mother stayed with the two younger children, while William and his father set out to do "man's work." William even rode with his father to London to buy their passage to Ireland.

On August 12, 1656, the Penn family climbed aboard the *Basing* for the trip. As they crossed St. George's Channel, the water was surprisingly calm, and William found himself enjoying the voyage more than he had imagined he would. His chest puffed out with pride when the ship's captain asked Admiral Penn's advice on different ways to tack or, in the evening, when the sailors gathered round and begged to hear stories of his famous naval battles. Nonetheless William was glad to set foot on dry land again. Although he enjoyed the experience of being at sea, it had not whetted his appetite for more.

William knew that Macroom was in the Irish countryside, which he imagined to be much like the countryside of Essex, where he had spent the happiest years of his childhood. He could not have been more wrong. Whereas Essex was peaceful and orderly, with small farmhouses dotted over the countryside and fat cows grazing on the rolling hills, Ireland looked like a war zone. Indeed it was. Since the English had invaded the country, one-third of the Irish population had been killed or maimed. And as their hired carriage rumbled through the green hills of southern Ireland, William saw countless burned houses and entire villages lying in ruin. When the coach stopped to water the horses, ragged children with tired eyes and pro-truding stomachs begged for food.

It was all too much for William, who pulled close to his mother inside the coach. Although he had studied some history in school, he could not understand why these people had to be put out of their homes and driven off their land. William knew better, however, than to discuss the matter with his father. As much as his father disliked Oliver Cromwell, he believed that the stronger nations should take over the weaker ones. And having done so, anything the stronger nations wanted should be theirs to take.

Everyone in the coach was glad when they arrived at Macroom Castle. Richard had cried and fussed most of the way, and everyone was relieved to finally be out of the carriage. The castle was just as huge as William had imagined. He stared up at its three-story-high gray stone walls. A small village of eight or ten huts crowded against the western wall.

"There'll be English peasants in there by the end of the month," Admiral Penn told William, pointing to the ramshackle village. "I'm having them sent out from Essex. They're harder workers than these Irish peasants."

William nodded, wondering what would happen to the families who lived in the village at present. Would they join those he had seen begging for food along the way?

Over the next several weeks, English Protestant peasants began arriving to work the land. William watched as his father evicted the Irish families from their tumbledown cottages and the English moved in. A company of foot soldiers and a horse brigade also arrived at the castle. Their job was to fend off any attacks from angry Irish Catholics.

Before long William's life fell into a pleasant pattern. He would study with his tutor in the morning and then straight after lunch help his father with the accounts and planning the farmwork. There was a lot to be done: New drainage ditches had to be dug, cattle needed to be fed, and seed for the various crops his father was experimenting with needed to be ordered. When that was over, William was free to climb on his horse and roam the countryside. He soon came to love the rugged land with its misty lowlands and high rocky cliffs.

One day, after the family had been living in the castle for about a year, the gatekeeper asked to speak to Admiral Penn. "Begging your pardon, sir," he said, "but I have it on good authority there is a Quaker on your land, stirring up trouble with the peasants and making all sorts of slanderous statements against God."

Twelve-year-old William's ears perked up. He had heard of the Quakers, a religious group of about forty thousand members in northern Europe who were hated by Protestants and Catholics alike. William also knew why they were called Quakers. George Fox, the group's founder, had said, "Thee will learn to *quake* before the word of the Lord," to a magistrate who was about to sentence him to prison. The magistrate scoffed and called George Fox and his friends Quakers. From then on the name for the group had stuck. William waited to see what his father would say about this Quaker man who had been spotted on the Penn estate.

"If you see him, tell him I will welcome him here, and he can hold a meeting with the household if he wants. There is plenty of meat and room here for one more. Goodness knows we should hear him out before we judge him. I know what it's like to be judged before you have a chance to defend yourself."

William was shocked to hear his father speaking this way. He assumed his father would have had the dogs sent after the man.

Two days later a servant announced a visitor. Thomas Loe was dressed simply in dark pants and dark jacket with a large, square white collar. On his head was perched a large black hat with a wide brim and slightly pointed top. Piercing blue eyes peered out from under the brim, yet Thomas's face was warm and open and his voice soft and kind. William liked him immediately, though he was surprised when Thomas did not doff his hat in deference when being introduced to his father. This was considered very bad manners, and William waited anxiously to see if his father would have the guest thrown out of the castle. Surprisingly Admiral Penn did not. Instead he led Thomas to the castle's great hall, where the household was gathered for a meeting.

When everyone was seated, Thomas Loe strode to the front of the great hall and began to speak.

> True religion is not a matter of outward observances. Rather it takes place within the heart. It is not rooted in past events in a far-off land but in the true Inner Light that shone then and continues to shine today. Men must follow this Inner Light until it illuminates their heart and they experience a closeness of God there. No other man, no priest or clergyman, can mediate this. Each man, in the quiet of his heart, must come to his own reckoning with God. For the Scriptures tell us that man looks on the outward appearance, but God looks at a man's heart.

As he spoke, Thomas's eyes rested on each person in the room, as though he were looking into their souls. He even set his intense gaze on Admiral

Penn, once again a show of bad manners. And once again the elder Penn did not appear to take offense.

Thomas went on to explain more of the basic beliefs of Quakers. As Thomas spoke, William found himself astonished by what he said. He had never heard anything like it before. All of his religious education to that point had come from attending the Church of England with his parents and from attending Chigwell School. Now a man, a scholar from Oxford University no less, was telling all these people that they could be in touch with God without the help of a clergyman or a prayer book or even the sacraments!

Transfixed, William took his eyes off Thomas long enough to look around the great hall. Jack, his father's black servant from Jamaica, was weeping aloud. And as William turned, he could see big tears spilling down his father's face. It was the first time he had seen his father cry, and the sight shocked him. Something in Thomas Loe's simple message was deeply moving, and the others in the room were feeling it as much as William was.

For nearly two years now William had been saying direct prayers to God, but he had not dared tell others lest they think he was crazy. Now a man was standing before him telling him it was fine to talk to God in this manner. You didn't need to be a priest to do so. Relief flooded through William; he was not crazy after all!

The next day Thomas Loe moved on, spreading the new religious message to whoever would listen, and life almost returned to normal for William.

Sometimes, though, William liked to sit on a rocky hillside and think about what Thomas had said. There were even times when he was sure an Inner Light was guiding his thoughts.

One year later, in September 1658, the Penns received the news they had been waiting for: Oliver Cromwell was dead! Amazingly, although he had made so many enemies, he had died of natural causes. Gossip quickly spread that Cromwell's funeral was a happy affair—the only ones crying were the dogs in the street outside! William's family was definitely happy about the turn of events. Mrs. Penn sang as she rehung the tapestries on the castle walls for winter, and Admiral Penn gave his peasants an extra day off.

Although Cromwell's son Richard had taken over his father's role as Lord Protector, Admiral Penn predicted he would not last long in power. It was Cromwell's daughters, not his sons, who had inherited their father's strong and ruthless streak. Indeed jokes began circulating about how the Cromwell men should wear the petticoats while the women wore the breeches!

William's father was right. Within eight months of his father's death, Richard Cromwell had been ousted from power. Now the Penn family waited anxiously in Ireland for news of who would fill the political power vacuum left in England.

Naval captains who were friends of the admiral often visited Macroom Castle. They brought with them news of the various men who were struggling to gain power in Britain. They told William and his father that English people were tired of army rule, tired of the uncertainty as to who would be their next leader, and especially tired of too much piety.

Finally, in March 1660, one of Admiral Penn's friends delivered a letter to him. It was from the mayor of Weymouth, and it invited the admiral to be Weymouth's representative in the new House of Commons. Things were starting to return to "normal." All that was needed now, William's father confided in him, was for someone to fetch King Charles's son back from exile in Holland.

"It is time to go home!" beamed William's father. "We've waited for four years, but our country has finally come to its senses and needs me once again."

Packing began immediately. Load upon load of silver plates, tapestries, pots, and other utensils were packed into crates for the voyage home. All the while William's mother worried about what the fashions would be like in London now that the Puritans were no longer enforcing their preference for drab colors. Four-year-old Richard chattered endlessly about traveling on a ship, and eight-year-old Margaret looked forward to meeting her Penn cousins back in England. But William thought he had the best reason of all to anticipate returning to England—his days of studying by himself were over. His father promised to enroll him at university upon their return home.

Chapter 4

A Bright Future

Two months later, in May, William Penn was standing amid an immense crowd that had gathered by the dock in Dover. It was unlike any other day people in England could remember. The whole of Dover was shut down for the huge event. Children laughed and played in the streets, and even the dogs that wandered about town wagged their tails more enthusiastically than normal. Twenty thousand horse and foot soldiers, brandishing their swords, lined the flower-strewn main street. The bells of the town's various churches rang out, and royal flags flew from every rooftop. Decorative tapestries had been hung in front of the houses that lined the streets, and people poured wine into the public fountains and drank from them.

William knew that since returning to London his father had been working quietly to bring Prince Charles back to England. It had required several tricky deals, including the Declaration of Breda, in which Charles promised that if he became king, he would abide by the new constitution Parliament had written. He also agreed to make peace with Oliver Cromwell's supporters, in particular the men who had killed his father the king, and allow Puritans to continue practicing their religion. When all this had been agreed to, the way was clear for Charles to return home. And now William stood waiting anxiously for him to arrive in Dover.

A small sloop had brought word ahead that Prince Charles was aboard the newly renamed *Royal Charles,* the flagship of the fleet of thirty-one ships that had gone to Holland to retrieve the Prince of Wales and declare him their new king. William's father, who had accompanied the fleet, along with several other members of Parliament, was also aboard the *Royal Charles.* Finally, when the massive flagship came into view, a deafening cheer went up from the crowd.

Less than an hour later, thirty-year-old Prince Charles stepped ashore. He was tall and dressed in a richly embroidered gown. When the crowd laid eyes on him, they went wild, calling out, "Long live Prince Charles."

Soon William spotted his father disembarking and ran to meet him.

"It is good to see you, boy," his father said. "I have some wonderful news!"

"I know, Father, I've seen Prince Charles already."

"Yes, yes, of course, but there is something else. Do you know the first thing His Highness did when he boarded the ship?"

"No," William replied.

Admiral Penn paused for dramatic effect, then said, "He commanded me to kneel, and he made me a knight."

"Sir William?" William asked. "You're Sir William Penn now?"

"That's right, boy," his father said, clapping him on the back. "What do you think of that? You are now the son of a nobleman, and I will make a way for you to follow me!"

William was so happy he laughed out loud. This time a year ago he had been exiled to a lonely outpost in Ireland. Now his father was at the center of England's new political power structure. The future had never looked brighter for William or his father.

William and his father joined the entourage of horses, soldiers, lords, politicians, and common people who accompanied the new king back to London.

In the months that followed, the Penns' spacious new residence on Tower Hill in London overflowed with important men. Even the duke of York, the new king's younger brother, came to visit. Soon afterward Sir William Penn announced to his family that he had been made commissioner of the navy by Parliament. He was now second in command of the British navy, under the lord high admiral, the duke of York.

Amid all of this excitement, William had new suits of clothes made, as well as a new flowing wig, so that he would look the part of a nobleman's son when he entered Oxford University in October.

Regrettably, King Charles II failed to keep his promise not to persecute those who had killed his father. William winced when he heard that some of Oliver Cromwell's generals were drawn and quartered at Charring Cross. More grotesque still was news that Parliament had voted for the body of Oliver Cromwell to be dug up from its resting place in Westminster Abbey, taken to the gallows, and hanged there, before being buried beneath the gallows. This form of revenge troubled William and made him more eager to get to Oxford, where he could submerge himself in books.

On October 26, 1660, two days after he turned sixteen, William finally got his wish. On that misty, gray day he stood outside the huge wooden doors of Christ Church College, Oxford. A sense of awe engulfed him. William knew that Charles I had stood on the exact same steps after he had fled London with his supporters and set up his new headquarters there. Oxford had opened the university's treasury to lend the beleaguered king money, and the buildings had been used to garrison loyal troops and store arms and as granaries and warehouses. Students had taken up arms in the king's cause, and musketeers had drilled on the quadrangles of the various colleges. The dean had even ordered that the silver plates from the dining room at Christ Church College be melted down and made into coins to pay the king's troops.

William was quickly welcomed inside the college and shown to his room on the second floor. As his newly assigned servant unfolded his clothes and hung them up, William looked out the window. He had never before seen such magnificent buildings, even in London. Gray stone structures dotted the landscape with magnificent archways and arcades, and a broad meadow flowed from the college down to the edge of the River Thames.

That night William walked into the dining hall at Christ Church College. He had dressed with extra care in a newly tailored red silk jacket with lace ruffled cuffs, white stockings and breeches, and a three-cornered hat. He surveyed the scene. The room, with its high vaulted ceilings and gothic arches, reminded him of a cathedral. Long tables ran the length of the hall, and at them sat the hundred or so other young students at Christ Church College. At the far end a table stretched across the hall, and at it sat the masters of the college, passing watchful glances over the young men in their care.

As William sat down at an empty place at one of the tables and looked around at his fellow students, his heart sank. To his left sat a group of four royalists, resplendent in their brightly colored jackets, Brussels lace, and long curly wigs. And on his right were two glum-faced young men wearing dark brown cassocks, with their hair cropped short—Puritans.

"Will we be seeing you out on the town tonight?" one of the royalist students asked in a mocking voice.

The two Puritans did not answer; instead they turned their attentions to the roast beef and cabbage set before them.

William recognized the same hatred and taunting that he had seen in London and that he disliked so much. And as his first week progressed, he came to see that this division between royalist supporters and Puritans infected everything that happened at the college. Each morning the sight of statues of saints with their faces smashed reminded William of the bitter battle that the country had been through.

When King Charles had fled from Oxford, Cromwell and his Puritan followers had moved through like a storm. They burned books that talked about royalty, smashed or defaced the statues of various saints, and looted any valuables they could find. It was said that Dean Samuel Fell, the college dean at the time, died of a broken heart when he saw what they had done to his college and heard that King Charles I had been executed.

After Charles I had fled, the Puritans had reigned supreme at Oxford. All sports and group events were canceled, and students were expected to study quietly and continuously. Cromwell had appointed Dr. John Owen as the new dean of the college. Dr. Owen was an unusual man and an odd choice for the Puritan government because he believed that a university should permit the open discussion of ideas! He believed that a university was not merely a place where students learned history and philosophy but a place where they could think about new discoveries. One such discovery recently made by Copernicus was that the sun and not the earth was the center of the universe. A second discovery by Tycho Brahe was that not all stars were ancient—some are still being formed. Men who studied astronomy and the physical sciences were invited to lecture at Oxford for the first time. Many royalist supporters thought this was scandalous, and they refused to send their sons to the university to hear such dangerous teaching.

When the royalists returned to power, the first thing they did was fire Dr. Owen and return lessons at Oxford to their "proper" order. When royalist leaders were sure that no more heresies were being taught, they began enrolling their sons again. However, these young students went wild as soon as they arrived. They partied on the town every night, and constant sports tournaments, plays, and feasts were carried on.

Meanwhile, royalists appointed John Fell, the son of Samuel Fell, to take his father's place as dean. The new Dean Fell, however, was a bitter man who was determined to stamp out any memory of the Puritans and reestablish the control of the Church of England. Older students told William that the dean expelled anyone who did not attend the Church of England chapel service every morning or who talked about Puritan ideals. The students even made up a taunt about the dean, which they recited behind his back: "I do not like thee, Dr. Fell. Why it is I cannot tell. But this I know and know full well: I do not like thee, Dr. Fell."

On William's first Saturday evening in Oxford, he walked into town to buy a new quill. It was dark, but he recognized a group of fellow royalist students standing around a lamp. He moved closer to see what they were doing.

"Go on, keep praying!" one of the students shouted. "Let's see if God will hear the prayers of a simpleton like you."

"Or should we call a priest and have him pray for you?" goaded another student.

William elbowed his way into the circle and looked down. There on the ground was a Quaker man in his early twenties. Blood oozed from a wound on the young man's forehead. A student kicked the man viciously in the side. "We'd drag you to the prison, but it's already filled with non-conformists!"

"Let's dunk him in the Thames instead!" another student yelled.

A cheer went up from behind William. As William turned he realized that a crowd of local people had now gathered to watch the "sport." Soon the students were dragging the Quaker down the muddy track to the riverbank. "One, two, three," they yelled in unison as they heaved him into the icy water.

William's first inclination was to dive in after him, but the Quaker splashed his way to the bank and started to climb out. As he did so, a student kicked him back into the river. "Come on, boys," he said gleefully, "let's go. There's plenty more fun where he came from."

Reluctantly, William turned and walked back toward town with the other students. He looked exactly like them on the outside, but inside he felt different. The Quaker reminded him of the excitement he had felt when Thomas Loe preached to his family in Ireland. Even though William was far from being a Quaker himself, he admired the simple, kind way they tried to live. He wondered what they had done to be hated so much.

With all thought of buying a new quill forgotten, William walked back to his dormitory. Although he had been at college only one week, it was long enough for him to know that he did not want to be friends with the other royalist students and that the Puritan students looked on him with suspicion because of who his father was. So William made a decision. He did not need any friends. He would keep his head down and study. After all, that was what he had come to Oxford to do.

Although his studies kept him busy, William did occasionally feel homesick. He was pleased, then, when his father sent money for him to catch a stagecoach back to London. In April 1661 most of his royalist classmates were headed that way, too, because Prince Charles was about to be crowned the new king of England there.

William found London brimming with excitement. Triumphal arches spanned the route of the royal procession from the Tower of London to Whitehall, and bright tapestries had been hung out the windows of the houses along the way.

On the morning of April 22 the Penn family rose early and dressed in their finest clothes. Soon they met up with another family, the Battens, and

Samuel Pepys and his wife. Together they made their way to the home of a flag maker in Cornhill. The procession would pass right in front of the house, and the group had been invited to watch the festivities from the house's second-story windows. As they sat waiting for the procession to begin, William's father formally introduced him to Samuel Pepys, their neighbor at the new house on Tower Hill. Samuel Pepys also worked at the Admiralty.

Finally the moment they had been waiting for arrived. The procession began winding its way past the house. First foot soldiers smartly clad in white doublets marched by, followed by soldiers on magnificently decorated horses. Then came Prince Charles himself, dressed in a richly embroidered suit and velvet cape. His brother, the duke of York, followed.

William's father put his hand on his son's shoulder as the two of them leaned forward to get the best view possible. It was then that the new king and his brother stopped in front of the house and looked up at Admiral Penn. They both raised their hands to him in a gesture of respect and honor. The admiral bowed in acknowledgment. William's chest puffed out with pride. He could scarcely believe it. King Charles II and the duke of York had both acknowledged his father. Could anything be greater in England than to have the honor and favor of the monarch?

"You have a bright future before you, boy. Be sure you make the most of it," Samuel Pepys assured William after the procession had passed.

Samuel Pepys was right. As the son of Sir William Penn, commissioner of the navy, William indeed had a bright future. With the favor his father enjoyed in the new royal court, William could easily become an adviser to the king or an ambassador in a foreign country when he graduated from Oxford. All he had to do was study hard at university and show himself to be a faithful royalist supporter.

Chapter 5

A Nonconformist at Heart

William Penn returned to Oxford determined to keep working hard and stay away from both Puritan and royalist students. However, avoiding them was not easy. Many of the courses he took involved discussion groups, and over time William discovered that most of the royalist students did not want to talk about politics or religion, two areas he had a great deal of interest in. By contrast, the Puritan students welcomed such discussions and often asked William what he thought. By the end of his first year at Oxford, an eyebrow-raising friendship between several Puritan students and William Penn, son of a royalist admiral, had begun to grow.

This friendship soon led William to Dr. Owen, the former dean of the university. Dr. Owen still lived nearby and held informal discussions in his living room. It was only a matter of time before William's new Puritan friends introduced him to these discussions, which soon became the highlight of his week. For the first time William was able to talk through his ideas with people who encouraged him in his thinking.

Two books he was reading particularly intrigued William. The first book was called *Oceana*, in which author James Harrington described an imaginary country where people lived together in freedom, cast ballots for their lawmakers, who served limited terms, and voted on their own laws. The other book was *International Law* by Hugo Grotius, which William read in Latin. Grotius imagined a world where kings and rulers were answerable for their subjects' welfare, where it was immoral for the king to declare war for personal gain or because of a personal grudge against another ruler, and where nations all worked together for peace. These ideas kept William awake at night trying to think of ways in which they could ever become a reality.

Dr. Fell, however, the current dean of the university, could not stand to have his old rival Dr. Owen leading students in "subversive" discussions and decided it was time to enforce the rules! Roll call was to be taken at chapel, and no one would be excused from attending. All students had to wear a surplice to class. This was a white gown that Church of England priests wore over their regular clothes. As well, Dr. Owen's house was strictly off-limits to all students.

Much to William's dismay, the whole climate of England was turning against those who would not buckle under to the Church of England. William's father and the other members of Parliament passed a new law a month after William returned to Oxford from the king's coronation. The law was called the Corporation Act, which declared that all men who held public office had to be members of the Church of England; everyone else—Catholics, Quakers, and nonconformists—was disqualified. This was the first of four acts that would come to be called the Clarendon Code.

Despite this changing climate, William was so excited with his newly formed thoughts on religion and politics that he did not care what the dean threatened him with. He was not about to stop visiting Dr. Owen in his spare time. Neither was he going to wear a surplice, the garb of a minister. He was a free human being, and he resolved that from now on he was going to be guided by his conscience and not a set of rules.

Before Christmas that year William received a written warning and a fine for his nonconformist behavior, but he reasoned he was at college to learn, not to be made into a Church of England priest. The battle of wits between William and Dr. Fell continued. William knew that no one wanted to expel him from Oxford—after all, he was not a Puritan but was the son of Sir William Penn, royalist member of Parliament. However, Dr. Fell decided it was time to clamp down even harder. On March 1, 1662, William Penn found himself standing outside the doors of Christ Church College surrounded by his luggage. He had been expelled from the school.

On the one-and-one-half-day coach trip back to London, William rehearsed ways in which to break the news to his father. He knew it would be a terrible blow to him, but he hoped his father would understand. His father did not!

"You what?" William's father boomed as his face turned bright red.

"I was asked to leave college," William replied quietly.

"You fool of a boy! What were you thinking? You had the world ahead of you, and you threw it away for some religious meeting. What is wrong with you? Do you know what you have done to me? This family is disgraced by your actions. What will the king do when he hears about this? Why, Parliament has ordered beheaded at least a dozen Puritans and their heads stuck on poles around the city as warning of what lies ahead for those who dare to disobey the law. Have you thought of that? Have you thought about anything?" screamed the elder Penn, his face so close to his son that William could feel the hot breath on his cheeks.

Crack! William felt the crushing pain of a fist across his face. He reeled backward and hit his head on the corner of the table. Thud! His father's fist smashed into his stomach, and William doubled over.

"I'll show you what I do to sailors on my ships who dare to disgrace me!" William Penn, Sr., bellowed, kicking his son in the ribs.

"Don't! Please don't," William heard his ten-year-old sister Margaret beg from the door.

"Get out and mind your own business!" roared Admiral Penn.

William sensed his moment to escape. He crawled to the doorway, pulled himself up, staggered out into the sunlight, and tumbled down the steps into the street. William's father stood in the doorway cursing at him as he stumbled away, blood running from his nose. William had absolutely no idea what to do next.

Eventually William arrived at a cheap inn, and the innkeeper's daughter agreed to bathe and bandage his wounds. William had a few coins in his purse to pay for lodging, though not enough for more than a week.

Two days later William's mother, Lady Penn, arrived at the inn. "I can't have a son of mine traipsing around London like a vagabond!" she exclaimed. "The neighbors are all asking questions about you, especially that nosey Mr. Pepys. I don't know what to tell them. Really, William, you should think about other people before you do these ridiculous things. Your father is the second highest-ranking naval officer in the country. You can't blame him for being angry with you. But he's calmed down now, and it's time for you to come home and apologize."

William did go home with his mother, but he refused to apologize. He did, however, try to explain to his father why he objected to being told he had to attend chapel and not to meet with Dr. Owen. His father simply did not understand. Since he became a sailor at age ten, he had been obeying or giving orders, and the thought of William doing something simply because his conscience told him to was unimaginable to him.

It soon became obvious that there was no use in talking, so William spent his days upstairs in his room. Servants brought his food and mail, and he rarely ventured downstairs into his father's domain. Despite his self-imposed exile in his room, bits of news filtered upstairs to William, most of it distressing. In May Parliament passed two acts into law. The first was called the Quaker Act. This act prevented Quakers from meeting together for worship in groups of more than five people. The penalties for violating the new law were tough. Fines were to be levied for first-time offenses, repeat offenders would be imprisoned, and lastly, those who refused to learn would be shipped to Jamaica and sold as slaves.

This law was quickly followed by the Act of Uniformity, which became part of the Clarendon Code. The Act of Uniformity insisted that religious leaders in England and Wales use the format for services found in the Church of England's Book of Common Prayer. Nearly two thousand ministers chose to quit their jobs rather than obey this law.

William could scarcely believe it. King Charles II had promised to be tolerant of other religious groups, but he had been outvoted on the issue by Parliament—which included William's own father! What was in store next for religious dissenters?

While William pondered the future for dissenters, he began to wonder about what lay in store for him as well. He found out in late June when his father announced he had booked William passage to France. "It will be a chance for you to start again," his father explained.

"Learning French manners will make you popular when you come home," his mother gushed.

So on July 6, 1662, William and his father traveled to Dover together. Sir William was on his way to Ireland to check on some newly acquired land, while eighteen-year-old William was bound for Paris, the most fashionable city in Europe. In his vest pocket William carried both a good supply of money and letters of introduction to some of the richest men in the city. Since it was too dangerous to travel alone, William's father had arranged for William to be a part of a group of distinguished English travelers, including his older cousin Robert Spencer, who were all on their way to Paris.

The journey was fast and uneventful, and before long William found himself walking the muddy streets of Paris. Thanks to the letters of introduction, he was soon invited into some of the wealthiest homes, where he was entertained in the most dazzling fashion.

Paris intrigued William; things were so different from London. When dining, guests used a fork as well as a knife, and the hostess did not appreciate it when the guests wiped their greasy hands on the overhanging tablecloth. In fact, the most fashionable of hostesses provided small squares of linen called napkins for the purpose. William had to constantly remind himself to use them.

Some aspects of life in Paris were very familiar to William, however. The social order was similar. People with money and title expected those without to pay them the correct homage. Hats had to be doffed at the appropriate times, knees bent, and respectful language used. It was a hat-doffing incident in Paris that showed William he was still a nonconformist at heart.

The incident happened late one night as William made his way home from a dinner party. A man doffed his hat to William and took immediate offense when William did not acknowledge the gesture. The truth was, on the dark street William had not noticed him remove his hat. The man drew his rapier and lunged at William, who dodged the thrust and drew his own sword. The two men parried backward and forward, each seeking to gain the advantage over the other. Finally William got the upper hand, and with a swift swipe of his sword, he knocked loose the man's rapier, which tumbled to the ground.

William moved in for the kill. It was customary for the victor in such a fight to drive his sword through his opponent's heart. As he raised his sword to do so, a thought raced through his head: What is a man's life worth? Was it worth a man losing his life in a simple disagreement over the doffing of a hat? William looked at the man and decided a life was worth far more than that. He put his sword back in its scabbard and let the man go.

During the following weeks, William Penn spent a lot of time thinking about the incident in the darkened street. He remembered many of the discussions he'd had with the Puritan students and with Dr. Owen. When he compared the excitement he had felt then with the glitter and extravagance of life in Paris, there was no comparison. Rather than live a life of privilege in Paris, William longed for the opportunity to explore ideas about religion and politics.

Around Christmas, William set out for the ancient town of Saumur, on the banks of the River Loire. Saumur was the home to L'Académie Protestante—the Protestant School. The school's principal was Moses Amyraut, a famous French theologian. From the moment he arrived, William loved the school and immediately enrolled himself in it. He hated to write and tell his father what he had done, but at least he was too far away for a beating.

At L'Académie Protestante William began a year of intellectual stretching and learning. He even stayed in Professor Amyraut's home and spent many hours talking with him about religious liberty and tolerance. However, in the spring of 1664 Moses Amyraut died. His death upset William a great deal, and William decided it was time to go home.

William arrived back in London in August 1664. His mother was delighted with the change in him. On the outside he was one of the most fashionable young men around. He spoke perfect French and had enough manners to charm any young woman he chose. But on the inside William was a very different person. The most important things he had learned in France were not the right way to spray perfume on his cuffs or how to use a napkin; rather, they were matters of the heart. William now had strong logical reasons for following his conscience, and that's what he intended to do, no matter what the consequences.

By now William's father knew how much William liked to argue about ideas, and he enrolled his eldest son at Lincoln's Inn. Lincoln's Inn was one of four Inns of Court in London where young men from rich and powerful families trained to be lawyers. William was eager to go, though for different reasons than his father imagined. Just before his return to London, Parliament had passed the Conventicle Act, the third part of the Clarendon Code. This new act made it illegal not just for Quakers but for any group other than the Church of England to gather for worship. William could not wait to get enough legal training so that he could help nonconformists prosecuted under this new law.

As William strolled along Chancery Lane and turned under the pointed Tudor arch into Lincoln's Inn, he was pleased about his unfolding future. He had a feeling he was going to enjoy studying to be a lawyer, and indeed he did. Within weeks he was participating in mock trials and discussing classic law texts by Dryden and Beaumont.

Toward the end of William's first year of study at Lincoln's Inn, England once again went to war against the Dutch, and Admiral Penn set sail with the British fleet. Soon afterward, in June 1665, a feeling of dread began to settle over London. The dread came not from the war with Holland but from the unusually high number of plague cases that were being reported in the city. Lincoln's Inn soon placed guards at its gates so that only students and teachers were admitted. But when one of the students came down with the telltale signs of shivering and vomiting, everyone was sent home.

William Penn hurried back to Tower Hill to check on his family.

Chapter 6

One Ray of Light

"Bring out your dead! Bring out your dead!" shouted a man leading a horse and two-wheeled cart through the narrow London streets.

For days now William Penn had been hearing the same cry and watched as grief-stricken people emerged from their houses carrying the bodies of family members. The bodies were loaded onto the cart and hauled away to be dumped in large mass graves that were dug at Greenwich.

At first it had been a thousand people a week dying from the disease, then two thousand a week. Before long there were over six thousand Londoners a week dying from the black plague. The smell of death was everywhere, and house after house had a telltale red cross, the sign of the plague, painted on the door.

Many of the rich families in London fled the city to the countryside, and the king moved the royal court out of the city. However, since William's father was away fighting the Dutch, Mrs. Penn and the children stayed on at their house at Tower Hill.

As William wandered through the streets of the stricken city, he was saddened by what he saw. The houses where cases of the plague had been confirmed were boarded up for forty days with the occupants inside. Often these frantic people starved or died of thirst before they were released.

Yet in all the darkness and gloom that hung over London in the summer of 1665, William noticed one ray of light. It came in the form of the Quakers, who smuggled food to those living in boarded-up homes, helped gather up the dead bodies for burial, and took in the orphans. This put the Quakers at great risk, and many of them caught the plague from those they were trying to help. These kind people's actions reminded William of something Moses Amyraut had told him during a discussion back at L'Académie Protestante in Saumur. The old professor had pointed out that piety alone was not enough, that morality dictates that a man must take responsibility to help his brother. And the Quakers, William observed, were doing just that. Their faith inspired them to reach out and help fellow human beings at a time of great need.

Yet even their humanitarian efforts did not spare the Quakers from persecution. Many of them were arrested and thrown into jail simply because they were trying to help. Rumors spread that Jews and Quakers were somehow responsible for the outbreak of the plague. Despite the persecution, the Quakers continued to help wherever they could. Some even carried a spare set of clothes with them in case they were arrested and sent to prison.

While the plague raged on and the Quakers went about helping victims of the disease, Parliament took the time to write the last of the four acts that made up the Clarendon Code. This new law, called the Five Mile Act, forbade any nonconformist preacher or teacher from coming within five miles of a city or town where he had served as a minister. William worried about what would happen to Dr. Owen under the law, since he had preached in Oxford and would no longer be welcome there.

In September William's father returned triumphant. The British had routed Holland's navy and seized many Dutch ships to add to their own fleet. However, the battle was Admiral Penn's last sea voyage. At forty-four years of age he was considered an old man, and the gout in his left leg was so painful that he could do little else but sit in the house with his leg propped up on a pillow. And the longer he sat with his leg propped up, the grumpier he became. Soon William was looking for somewhere to go to get away from him.

In October William turned twenty-one, the age at which he could legally represent his father, and this gave him an idea. He suggested that he go to Ireland and complete the transfer of title to some new land King Charles II had given to the admiral.

William's father thought this was a wonderful idea. After spending a quiet Christmas with his family, William set out for Cork, Ireland, in January 1666.

William was glad to be away from London. He breathed in deeply the crisp sea air that blew through St. George's Channel. The air smelled salty and sweet, unlike the fetid stench of death that still hung over London. Indeed, by now the plague had claimed more than seventy thousand lives.

It had been seven years since William was last in Ireland. He had left as a boy and was returning as a well-educated and well-traveled young man. Once again letters of introduction opened doors to the small but elite group of English noblemen in Ireland. And when William was not settling claims with tenants or wading through endless paperwork, he spent his time in Dublin with dukes and earls.

In June 1666 a garrison of King Charles's soldiers was stationed at Carrickfergus, the stone fortress that guarded the harbor of Belfast Lough. Dissatisfied with their conditions, the entire garrison mutinied, and the earl of Arran called for volunteers to restore order in the area. William rushed to sign up.

Once order was restored, William took time to have his portrait painted in Dublin. He borrowed a suit of armor to wear for the sitting, knowing his father would like to see him dressed in fighting gear. William then went back to managing his father's estate. However, letters from home told him things were not dull there. Fifteen-year-old Margaret was being courted by a suitably rich young man named Anthony Lowther. It sounded as if a wedding was in the air.

Then more news came, this time devastating. As if the people of London had not suffered enough through the plague, a huge fire had sped through the city. William listened as reports of the fire reached Ireland. It had started on September 2, when a baker in Pudding Lane did not properly extinguish the fire in his oven. Sparks from the fire ignited firewood stacked nearby, and soon the baker's whole house was ablaze. At first people were not too worried. Most houses in London were built of wood and had thatch roofs, and it was not uncommon for a spark to ignite a house fire. Usually the fire was extinguished before it spread too far, but not this time. The wind combined with an extremely dry summer made conditions ideal for the fire to spread quickly up Pudding Lane and across the whole city of London.

By the time the fire was put out three days later, it had destroyed four-fifths of the city. Over thirteen thousand homes and ninety churches were burned. Miraculously, only sixteen people lost their lives in the blaze. William was relieved to hear that the family home at Tower Hill had been spared. The fire had spread westward, avoiding the eastern side of the city where the Penn house was located.

After hearing of the tragedy in London, William was eager to see his family again. When he heard that Margaret was to be married in late February 1667, he booked passage for home.

As William rode through the streets of London on his way to Tower Hill, he could scarcely believe his eyes. Although the Fire of London had occurred over four months before, the city still lay in ruins. The charred skeletons of buildings lined what were once thriving streets, and people were forced to live in tents. In several places William noticed that the rebuilding effort was getting under way. This time the buildings were being constructed from brick and stone rather than wood and thatch in an effort to limit the effects of possible future fires.

Despite the devastation, one good side effect had resulted from the fire. Since the blaze, the black plague that had scourged the people of London for well over a year suddenly disappeared. No one knew why it did, but everyone was glad to finally be rid of it.

As he rode along William thought about all that he had learned from Moses Amyraut. He saw how pointless it was accumulating so many possessions. A single spark could take them all away. No, he told himself, there were more important things in life than social position and an abundance of possessions for him to strive for.

William did not enjoy his sister's wedding. Margaret had changed a lot since he had last seen her. She was preoccupied with the gilded coach that Anthony Lowther had given her and with her new servants. She was so interested in socializing with other rich young couples that she hardly noticed or cared about the devastation all around her. To make matters worse, their father's gout was no better and seemed to make him more short-tempered than ever.

William escaped back to Ireland as soon as he could. Not long after arriving in Ireland, he rode into Cork to buy some new clothes. He went in search of a drapery shop and finally found a small one tucked in a back alley. As he entered the store, the first thing he noticed was the woman behind the counter. She was a Quaker, clad in a simple cotton dress and apron. "I greet you, ma'am," William said.

"And you also," the woman replied, looking him directly in the eye.

There was something about her honest look that reminded William of everything he admired in the Quakers he had met.

"I doubt you would be needing anything in here," the woman went on, looking at William's frilly cuffs and embroidered velvet vest. "We sell plain things."

William smiled at her. "Well, sometimes plain things are the best things," he said, watching as the woman's eyebrows raised. No doubt she was thinking his reply a strange thing for a rich young nobleman to say. He went on, "I once had the good fortune to hear a Quaker such as yourself. He came to my father's home and spoke to the entire household."

"And what was his name?" the woman asked, looking a little more relaxed.

"Thomas Loe," William replied. "I have never heard a man who had such a peaceful countenance.

Why, I would walk one hundred miles just to hear him speak once again."

The woman stared at William for a long time and then lowered her voice. "You do not have to walk that far. Thomas Loe is holding a secret meeting not three miles from here tonight. I am going myself, and if you like, I will take you with me," she said in a conspiratorial whisper.

William's mind reeled. It was one thing to confess to a Quaker woman that he would like to hear Thomas Loe speak, but being confronted with the opportunity to do so was quite a different matter. The Clarendon Codes made it both illegal and dangerous to have anything to do with the Quakers. The penalty for violating the law and associating with Quakers was imprisonment or worse, being deported to the West Indies and sold as a slave.

After debating the issue in his mind for a few moments, William decided he had nothing to worry about. Most of the Quakers he knew were lowly folk with little education or social rank. By contrast, he was a gentleman, the oldest son of Britain's naval hero Sir William Penn, no less. There was no way he would be in danger, even if he were caught attending a Quaker meeting. No constable or court employee would dare hold him in jail.

With the assurance of his safety settled in his mind, William replied, "I would like very much to attend the meeting with you. What time shall I return to your store?"

"Six o'clock," the woman replied. "My husband will be here then, and we will all go together."

Twenty-two-year-old William Penn did not know it then, but he had just arranged a date with destiny.

Chapter 7

Walking Unarmed in an Armed World

William Penn followed the shopkeeper and her husband through the darkened back alleys of Cork to a small wooden house. Inside, illuminated by several candles sat a group of Quakers. William smiled at their startled faces when he walked in. He knew how out of place he looked to them.

As the meeting began, William's heart thumped in his chest. Everyone sat expectantly in silence, waiting for someone to be moved to speak, read a passage from the Bible, or pray aloud. After several minutes an old man stood up. He looked around the room and then began speaking in a quiet, firm voice. William recognized his voice immediately. It was Thomas Loe, though he had aged a great deal in the years since they had last met.

"There are two types of faith people can have," Thomas began. "The first is the type of faith that overcomes the world. The second is a faith that is overcome by the world. The question we must each ask ourselves is, which type of faith do we have?"

Once again William found himself spellbound by the words of this preacher. Halfway through the talk he felt he had to do something to show how deeply moved he was. William stood up and remained standing, not worrying what the others in the room thought of him. Soon tears were running down his cheeks and onto his frilly collar.

When the meeting was over, Thomas and William talked long into the night. Everything the preacher said made perfect sense to William. Faith—real faith—was not about the things in this world but was about the things that cannot be seen: love and peace and following the light of a conscience illuminated by Jesus Christ. Religion was a matter for an individual's heart and not a matter for governments. Kings and rulers mock true religion when they use it as a tool to strengthen their power over their citizens.

By the time William went to bed that night he felt exhilarated, something he had not felt since sitting by the fireside talking with Dr. Owen in Oxford and Moses Amyraut in France. While William had not made a decision to become a Quaker—that was something that required a lot of thinking through—he was what Thomas Loe called a "seeker of truth." And where his search for truth would lead him, William was not sure.

Over the following months William attended many secret Quaker meetings around Cork, sitting in silence, listening to preachers, and mulling over what religion was really about. William knew that in the end he would have to decide whether he would officially become a Quaker. However, he did not know that this decision would be made in a public and dramatic manner.

On a cool Saturday evening, September 3, 1667, William walked into a Quaker meeting being held in the upstairs room of a house in Cork. By now everyone gathered was used to having the finely dressed young man worship among them. Those present were just beginning a time of silence when the downstairs door swung open. Soon they heard footsteps on the stairs, and a single soldier burst into the room. "Ah, I thought this is where you all gathered!" he exclaimed, pulling a dagger from his vest. "All of you, line up against that wall."

William looked around the room to see what the other nineteen people would do. Slowly the Quakers got up and moved. Several of them bowed their heads in prayer as they did so. William fumed inside. This was not good enough! What right did a soldier have to come into a private house and disrupt a meeting? It was an outrage.

Before he had thought it through, William jumped up and ran over to the soldier. "How dare you!" he bellowed at the shocked man. Then he grabbed the soldier by his collar. The soldier's dagger clattered to the floor. William then pulled the man toward the stairs. The man kicked and fought, but he was no match for William's strong arms.

When he got to the top of the stairs, William lifted the man high, ready to throw him down.

"No, brother, don't!" said one of the Quakers. "It's not our way. We will not meet violence with violence. No man will come to ill in my home."

William paused. Everything inside of him wanted to throw the man down the stairs and hope he broke his neck, but the Quaker way was a way of peace and love, even in the midst of hatred. "You are right," he finally said, putting the soldier down.

As soon as his feet hit the floor, the soldier bolted down the stairs and out the door.

"He will be back with others," William said gloomily.

"Maybe, or maybe not," replied the homeowner. "It is in God's hands. Let us continue our meeting."

Twenty minutes later everyone heard the door open again. This time it was not one set of footsteps on the stairs but fifteen.

"Everyone put your hands on your head!" yelled a soldier as a group of men surged into the room.

This time William did not try to resist but did as he was asked.

Soon nineteen Quakers and William Penn were standing before the mayor of Cork, who looked gravely at them. A shocked look overtook his face when he saw William. "Release that prisoner," he said, pointing at William. "Someone has obviously made a mistake. This man is not a Quaker. In fact, he is the lord of a castle."

The mayor looked directly at William. "Sir," he said, "accept my humblest apologies and the apologies of the court. You have been arrested in error, and you are free to go." He then turned to a soldier. "Lock the rest in jail, and I'll deal with them on Monday."

William stood in the midst of his new friends. They were on their way to jail, and he was a free man. He felt the palms of his hands get sweaty. What should he do? Could he live with himself if he left the others there and went back to his castle and his servants? Who were his people? The royalists, who thought it was fine to arrest a person for having a private religious meeting in his own home, or the Quakers, who believed that every man and woman had a right to follow their own inner light?

Drawing himself up to his full height, William spoke in a clear, respectful voice. "Lord Mayor, I beg to differ with you. I am indeed a man of wealth. My father, as you well know, is Admiral Sir William Penn. But know this as well: I am also a Quaker, and whatever you plan to do to my friends I ask you to do to me also."

The room fell deathly quiet. The mayor turned white. "I have no quarrel with you, Mr. Penn," he said in a shaking voice. "I am not sure you heard me right. *You are free to go.*"

William shook his head. "I am not sure you heard me right. I said I am a Quaker, and I wish to remain with the others. What is more, as an Oxford scholar and a member of Lincoln's Inn, I wish to argue our case. Please tell me on what charges we are being held here."

The mayor's face hardened. "Very well, if that is the way you want it. You are charged with being present at a tumultuous and riotous assembly."

"And what act is that a part of?" William asked.

"The Quaker Act," the mayor replied briskly. "But this is not a trial. I have already been dragged out at this late hour. To the cells with all of you. I will see you again on Monday." With that the mayor beckoned for the soldiers to take the prisoners away.

A crowd had gathered outside the building. They jeered and threw stones as the Quakers were led away. Just as the group reached the threshold of the jail, William realized he was still wearing his sword. He stopped and unbuckled it. The rubies and sapphires that encrusted the sword's handle gleamed in the light of the torches the soldiers carried. The throng grew silent as William stepped out of the group and walked over to a young male bystander. He bowed to the young man and offered him the sword. "Take this," he said. "From now on I will walk unarmed in an armed world."

The shocked young man took the sword. William smiled at him and then turned and walked into the Cork jail. He was in prison for the first time in his life, yet inside he felt freer than ever. His heart was filled with joy.

The following day William asked for paper and a quill so that he could write a letter to the earl of Orrery, the lord president of the province. He thought for a long time before he began, and then he wrote:

Religion, which is at once my crime and mine innocence, makes me a prisoner of a mayor's malice, but mine own free man...I hope your lordship will not now begin an unusual severity, by indulging so much malice in one, whose actions savor ill with his nearest neighbors, but that there may be a speedy releasement to all for attending their honest calling...and though to dissent from a national system imposed by authority renders men heretics, yet I dare believe your lordship is better read in reason and theology, than to subscribe to a maxim so vulgar and untrue.

The more William wrote, the more energized he became. He went on to point out that the Quakers were a religious group, not a political one, and that they were committed to nonviolence and posed no threat to the government.

The letter worked. No charges were brought against the group, and they were free to go back to their normal lives, except that William's life was now anything but normal. He had gone to the meeting as a seeker of truth and come home from the jail a Quaker.

William continued to attend meetings and read everything he could about Quakers. All the while he waited for the inevitable—a letter from his father. Finally, in late October, the letter arrived, and William opened it with trembling hands and read.

Son William: I hope this will find you in health. The cause of this writing is to charge you to repair to me with all possible speed, presently after your receipt of it, and not to make any stay there, or any place upon your road, until it pleases God you see me (unless for necessary rest and refreshment). Your very affectionate father, W. Penn.

There it was. Obviously William's father had heard about his imprisonment and acceptance of Quakerism, and now William was being summoned home to face his father over the matter. It was a scary prospect. Thankfully, a Quaker preacher named Josiah Coale offered to go with William. Josiah also came from a wealthy family and was no stranger to persecution. In fact he had been imprisoned many times before and beaten by mobs in both Ireland and England. He had even traveled to the New World, where he had been banished from Maryland for preaching. From there he had traveled on to Jamaica and then to Holland to encourage Quakers in exile there.

William hastily organized the affairs of his father's estate and set sail with Josiah for England. He was glad of the reassuring company of Josiah in the inevitable confrontation that lay ahead.

The Penns had moved from the still charred remains of London back to Wanstead, which is where William and Josiah headed. As the two men climbed from the carriage, neither of them doffed his hat, something that previously William did automatically. William watched his father's face grow red with anger at the apparent lack of respect.

"So what I have heard is true," William Penn, Sr., growled.

"Yes, Father," William replied. "I am a Quaker."

The three men talked into the night, and for most of the time, Sir William managed to keep his temper under control. William suspected it was because Josiah was in the room with them. That's why his father's last words that night were so ominous to William. "Be ready at seven o'clock tomorrow morning. You and I are going out in the coach—alone."

"Yes, Father," William said quietly.

As he lay in bed that night, William had no idea what would happen to him the next morning. Where was his father taking him? Would he become violent as he had when William was expelled from Oxford?

William had no difficulty waking up at six the next morning. He had not slept a wink all night. He was too busy worrying about what his father might do. He dressed and crept downstairs. Sure enough, his father was waiting for him. Barely a word was said as the two men ate their breakfast and stepped into the family carriage.

"Drive us to the park," Sir William Penn ordered the coachman.

"I can scarcely believe what you are doing," the elder Penn said to his son in a controlled voice. "I doubt you have thought through all the implications of this foolish act."

William sat silently, and his father went on. "I have made sure you had the best education possible. You have been trained up to be an ambassador or a member of Parliament. How could you possibly give it all up for this ridiculous notion?"

"It is not ridiculous to me, Father," William replied. "I became a Quaker out of obedience to God and my conscience. And I know you understand what I mean by that. Did not you yourself weep when you heard Thomas Loe preach in our home in Ireland?"

"No, you are wrong," his father snapped. "There is no way I can understand a bright young man such as you throwing your life away. Do you understand that the king is now bent on repressing all nonconformist religions? For a while it was the Parliament who led the fight, but now the king is as determined as the rest of us to wipe out nonconformists. He is still angry that Cromwell's forces beheaded his father, and he will not allow a movement like Cromwell's to take root in this country again. Mark my words, son, Quakers are about to be crushed under the hand of the king. I know him well, and when he needs to be ruthless, he is. If you continue in this manner, not even I, with all my contacts, will be able to protect you from the consequences. In fact, I suppose you will lose your life and I my career for raising such a son as you."

William continued to listen. What could he say? Certainly nothing that would change his father's mind. Nor could his father say anything that would change William's mind. They were both locked into their positions, and a great gulf separated them.

Eventually the coach rumbled past a tavern, and the men stopped and ordered mulled wine. Sir William asked for it to be served to them in a private room upstairs. As soon as the wine was delivered, he walked over to the door. William heard the key turn in the lock and braced himself for a beating. Much to his surprise, his father walked over to the table and laid his hands on it and in a trembling voice announced, "I am going to kneel down and pray that God will save you from becoming a Quaker."

William was horrified by the idea that his father would pray that way. Without thinking he flung open the window shutters and turned to his father. "You will see me jump from this window before I allow you to do that!" he said.

Father and son stood defiantly, their eyes locked. Several minutes passed, and then there was a knock at the door. Sir William unlocked the door and opened it. Standing outside was a member of Parliament. "Ah, Sir William," the man said heartily, "I saw your coach outside and decided to stop for a drink with you. How are you?"

The moment had passed. William and his father played host to the nobleman, and when he left they climbed back into the carriage. William's father had not prayed for him, and William had not jumped from the window.

In the days that followed, the two men fell into an uneasy truce. William tried to avoid his father whenever possible and spent most of his time in London with other Quakers. Inevitably he was arrested at another secret meeting, and although he was not charged, the magistrate sent a letter informing Sir William Penn what his son had been up to.

Once again William was summoned to his father's side at Wanstead. This time, however, it was not for a discussion. Instead William's father informed him that he had gone too far this time. There was nothing to talk about.

"You are to pack your bags," he said coldly, "and remove every reminder of yourself from this house. I do not want to see you again. I am going to write you out of my will and give my estate to someone who pleases me better."

With a sad heart William packed his bags. His mother stood at the door weeping. William gave her one final hug and walked out of the house. At twenty-four years of age, William Penn was both homeless and penniless, but he was far from friendless.

Chapter 8

A New Opportunity

William sat quietly as the coach left Wanstead behind, along with the security and promise he had known all his life. There would be no inheritance for him now, no estate in Ireland, no orchestrated introductions to young women who might make a suitable wife for the son of a nobleman, and no fine dinners with members of Parliament. Yet the loss of these privileges did not burden William's heart. In fact William felt as if a tremendous weight had been lifted off him. Gone with all the privileges were also the responsibilities of his heritage. He no longer had to worry about embarrassing his father or not dressing stylishly enough for his mother. And he no longer had to manage the family estate in Ireland that he would have inherited.

William realized that he had an opportunity few other members of his social class ever enjoyed—the chance to do whatever he wanted without worrying about what other people thought. And William knew just what it was he wanted to do. He wanted to use his education and background to help the Quaker movement.

Josiah Coale took William to a Quaker friend's house, and right away William began arranging a meeting with the duke of Buckingham. The duke was an old friend of the Penns and one of the most powerful men in the royal court. A meeting with the duke was granted, and William invited three of the most influential Quaker leaders to join him: Thomas Loe, George Whitehead, and Josiah Coale.

At the meeting the four Quakers told their stories. Josiah had just been released from prison, Thomas was newly returned from Ireland, where he had been beaten many times, and George had been incarcerated in Marshalsea Prison in Southwark. Along with their stories, William spoke of the many other groups who were being persecuted for their religious beliefs. One of these men was the dissenter John Bunyan, who had been in prison for eight years. Unfortunately, the duke would not help them. He told them he understood their problem, but he was not willing to put his own life on the line for dissenters. They knew the law, and they could either abide by it or suffer the consequences.

William was discouraged by the outcome of the meeting, but he was far from giving up. Instead he looked for another way to help his new cause.

George Fox, the founder and leader of the Quakers, was a gifted and inspiring speaker but not much of a writer. As a weaver's son he'd had little opportunity for formal learning. William saw his chance. He knew that with his legal training and writing skills, he could write tracts that would help people understand the Quakers' true message and replace the ignorance that led to much of the persecution they faced.

William had just one problem. Everything printed in England had to be approved by the government censors, and stiff fines were levied against anyone who published unapproved materials. Josiah Coale, though, thought William's idea was brilliant and found an underground printer who was prepared to publish whatever William wrote.

William's writing career began with two tracts, one entitled *Truth Exalted* and the other *The Guide Mistaken*. The tracts were circulated among Quaker families in England and Ireland and were widely used to help seekers find their way. Immediately William Penn found himself a household name among Quakers, and many families invited him to visit them. One such invitation came in the summer of 1668 from Isaac and Mary Penington, a wealthy couple who lived in a huge home called The Grange, in Chalfont St. Peter in Buckinghamshire.

While visiting The Grange, William met Gulielma Springett, Isaac Penington's stepdaughter. Gulielma's father, Sir William Springett, had been one of Oliver Cromwell's generals. He had died shortly before Gulielma was born, and several years later Gulielma's mother, Mary, had married Isaac Penington.

William liked Gulielma, or Guli, as she preferred to be called, from the start. She had a warm, open face, sparkling blue eyes, and curly blond hair. But more than her looks, William was impressed with her mind. Unlike most women of the day, Guli was well educated and well read. The two of them talked together for hour upon hour. In fact, instead of staying one night at the Penington house as he had planned, William ended up staying five nights. And at the end of his stay, William Penn was sure of one thing: He wanted to get to know Guli Springett better.

Over the summer, while William was visiting Quaker families, one of his tracts fell into the hands of a Presbyterian pastor named Thomas Vincent, who pastored a church in Spitalfields. Thomas Vincent became incensed at what he read and began denouncing William and the Quakers from his pulpit. When William heard this, he wrote to Thomas asking for the opportunity to have an open debate with him regarding Quaker beliefs. At first the Presbyterian pastor was reluctant, but he finally agreed to a debate to be held at two in the afternoon on August 31, 1668.

William, accompanied by George Whitehead, arrived at the church for the debate, only to find that Thomas had started the meeting at one o'clock and used the first hour to barrage his congregation with a sermon on the evils and dangers of Quakers. The stirred-up crowd booed and jeered when William and George entered the church.

It soon became obvious to William that it was not a fair debate. When he and George tried to explain Quaker beliefs, Thomas Vincent cut them short. The whole atmosphere soon took on that of an inquisition. Rather than let the men explain themselves, Thomas resorted to telling the two Quakers why their theology was wrong and calling them blasphemers. The crowd delighted in the name calling and hurled their own abusive names at William and George. Still, the two Quakers stood their ground, unwilling to concede any of the points on which Thomas challenged them.

The meeting dragged on for hours, and darkness fell outside, until abruptly and rudely Thomas stormed out of his church, leaving William and George at the mercy of the crowd. The two Quakers tried to address the congregation directly, but the scene soon became ugly. Some of the men grabbed William and George and manhandled them outside into the dark.

After his visit to Thomas Vincent's church, William could not stop thinking about the arguments he would like to have made if the crowd had listened. This spurred him on to write his next tract, which he titled *The Sandy Foundation Shaken*. This tract caught the attention of church leaders in a way that William's previous tracts had not. Within days of its publication, William Penn found himself rounded up and escorted to his new home—a cell in the Tower of London.

While William was held on charges of illegally publishing a tract, it was the content of the tract that really got him in trouble. The bishop of

London had read the tract and saw it as a direct challenge to church theology and his authority. All high church officials at the time had the right to arrest anyone they thought went against established beliefs, and so on December 12, 1668, William was ordered arrested by the bishop and taken to the tower.

William had been born near the Tower of London. The Penn family still owned a house nearby. William had walked past the Tower many times, had even played within its shadow as a child. His father had been imprisoned there by Oliver Cromwell, but he had never imagined being a prisoner there himself.

As he was led to the top of the large square, squat stone tower where his cell was located, William passed the chambers where various tortures had been used on prisoners. There was the dark chamber where in times past people had been tied to the rack and suffered in agony until they admitted their crime or their body was pulled apart by the wretched device. And there was the chamber where men were laid between two boards and rocks were piled on top until they confessed. And if they refused to confess, their tormentors would pile on more rocks until the weight of them crushed their chest. And now this infamous place was William Penn's new home!

As William sat in his cell, shivering from the winter cold that seeped through the tower roof above his cell, he felt truly alone for the first time in his life. He was allowed no visitors and no contact with the outside world. Finally a note was delivered to him from the bishop of London. It read, "Recant in Common Garden at an appointed time before all the City, or else be a prisoner for life."

Deep down William knew he could not deny the Quaker faith. It simply made too much sense to him, and if he denied it, he would be ignoring his own conscience. So he wrote back to the bishop: "Thou mayst tell my father, whom I know will ask thee, these words, that my prison shall be my grave before I will budge a jot, for I owe my conscience to no mortal man. I have no need to fear. God will make amends for all."

William also wrote a letter to Lord Arlington, Principal Secretary of State. He pointed out that he had not been brought to trial and had not been able to defend himself, both of which made his imprisonment illegal under British law. William finished the letter by saying, "I make no apology for my letter as a trouble—the usual style of suppliants; because I think the honor that will accrue to thee by being just and releasing the opprest, exceeds the advantage that can succeed to me."

William was smart enough, however, to understand that both King Charles II and Parliament were in a difficult position. If they brought him to trial and allowed him to speak in his own defense, what he said would be reported all over England, strengthening Quaker views and turning William into a martyr. And if they simply let him go, the bishop of London would lose face and other Quakers would be emboldened to speak out the message that the church had no authority over a man's soul. They had only one solution: Keep things the way they were. And that is what happened. Month after month William remained in the cramped cell at the top of the Tower of London.

Thankfully, William was eventually allowed a quill and paper to continue his writing. He spent his days thinking about the situation he was in and all of the writers down through history he had studied at Oxford and in France under the guidance of Moses Amyraut. Eventually William began to write down what he was thinking. With only the aid of his memory, he quoted sixty-four different authors, from Socrates to Martin Luther, and four hundred passages from the Bible in another essay about Quaker beliefs. He called this essay *No Cross, No Crown*, and promised himself that he would find a way to smuggle it out of the tower.

Soon after he finished writing the essay, William received the first visitor to his cell—Dr. Edward Stillingfleete, one of the royal chaplains. On his first visit, Dr. Stillingfleete tried to persuade William to do as the bishop of London wanted and renounce his Quaker beliefs. By the third visit he had given up on that tack. Instead Dr. Stillingfleete listened to what William had to say. And as he listened, he began to see that what the bishop of London had categorized as blasphemy and a direct challenge to the church's authority was in fact a misunderstanding. William had failed to fully explain his beliefs in *The Sandy Foundation Shaken*. This gave Dr. Stillingfleete an idea of how to end the impasse and get William freed from jail. He suggested that William write a second tract that explained more fully the beliefs laid out in *The Sandy Foundation Shaken.*

William agreed that he could expand on what he had written and explain things better, but he would not change any of his beliefs. So with Dr. Stillingfleete's blessing, he set to work.

When William was finished writing the new tract, which he titled *Innocency with Her Open Face* and which carried a subtitle declaring that the tract was "presented by Way of Apology for the Book Entitled *The Sandy Foundation Shaken,*" Dr. Stillingfleete presented it to King Charles. The king was grateful to finally have a dignified way to end William's imprisonment. As head of the Church of England, King Charles II persuaded the bishop of London that the tract was the best apology he was going to get from William and that it was time to release William Penn from jail. On July 28, 1669, William's cell door swung open, and William was once again a free man.

Chapter 9

A Tumultuous Proceeding

William Penn soon found out that he was not as free as he thought he was. His release from the Tower of London had conditions, one of which was that his father be responsible for him for one year. Sir William Penn soon told his son he wanted him back in Ireland looking after the family estate there. This would get William out of the tense political situation in London. William had little choice but to obey his father, though he did plan a stop along the way to Ireland.

The stop was at the Peningtons' home. While imprisoned in the Tower of London, William had spent many hours thinking about Guli Springett, and he was eager to see if she still remembered him. He need not have worried. Guli, along with her whole family, was glad to see William again.

While he was in jail, their beautiful manor house, The Grange, had been confiscated because they were Quakers, and now the Peningtons lived nearby it in a modest farmhouse. This did stop them from offering the same gracious hospitality to William as they had done before.

William stayed with the Peningtons for five days, attending many meetings with Guli. During this time his and Guli's affection for each other grew, until William had a feeling that one day Guli would be his wife.

At one of the Quaker meetings he attended with Guli, William met Philip Ford, a merchant with a good reputation. Philip was looking for a new job, and William was looking for a man to help him manage his father's estate in Ireland. The two men appeared to be a good match, and William hired Philip on the spot. Guli's fourteen-year-old half brother, John, also wanted to go with William to Ireland. So on October 23, 1669, the eve of William's twenty-fifth birthday, the three men set sail for Cork, Ireland.

Once in Ireland, William went straight to work, both looking after his father's estate and trying to help Irish Quakers, particularly the hundreds who were in prison around the country. He made repeated calls on the rich and influential English-men living in Ireland, challenging them to give the Quakers their freedom. Eventually his persistence paid off. The Lord Lieutenant of Ireland called for the release of all Quaker prisoners being held because of their beliefs.

In July 1670, certain that his father's land was being well looked after, William felt confident enough to return to London and report to his father. On August 1, nine months after arriving in Ireland, William and John boarded a ship for London, while Philip stayed behind to manage the Penn estate.

William arrived in London just as a scandal was brewing. The British Parliament had joined with Holland and Sweden, two other large Protestant European nations, in what was called the Triple Alliance. This alliance was put together to keep Catholic France from becoming stronger and taking over any more territory. However, behind Parliament's back King Charles II had secretly signed the Treaty of Dover, pledging to become a Catholic himself and return England to Roman Catholicism. Not only that, he had pledged to assist France in a war against Holland.

When the country learned of the king's treachery, people were furious, and none more so than the members of Parliament! They dusted off the Conventicle Act and added some new teeth to it. Now anyone over sixteen years of age who attended a non–Church of England religious meeting was subject to fines and imprisonment. While this law was designed once and for all to put down the power of the Catholic Church in England, it mostly hurt the Quakers and other dissenter groups.

Preachers were being dragged off to prison in larger numbers than ever, and religious meetinghouses were boarded up. On August 14, 1670, William arrived at a meetinghouse on Gracechurch

Street in London to attend a Quaker gathering. When he found the building boarded up and sol- diers standing guard outside, William suggested to the other Quakers that they move a little way down the street to a corner and hold a prayer service there. Within a few minutes William and another man, William Mead, were arrested and marched off to Newgate Prison.

After two weeks in jail, on September 1, William Penn and William Mead were brought before Sir Samuel Starling, lord mayor of London and the highest-ranking municipal judge in the city. The trial was held at Old Bailey, London's criminal courts building, located adjacent to Newgate Prison.

As he entered the court, William looked around at the inside of the old building. The walls were stone and paneled with dark timber. High gothic arches supported the roof, and leaded windows set high in the walls let shafts of hazy light into the room. Together, the coldness of the stone walls, the darkness of the paneling, and the shafts of muted sunlight created an effect of ominous gloom that hung over the court. The two defendants were led into the raised dock that faced the bench where the lord mayor, the court recorder Thomas Howell, and several aldermen sat. The jury of twelve men were then brought in, and an oath was adminis- tered to them.

It was time to start prosecuting the case. The court recorder began to read aloud the indictment against the two men.

That William Penn, Gent., and William Mead, late of London, Linen-draper, with divers other persons to the jurors unknown, to the number of three hundred, the 14th day of August, in the 22nd year of the King. About eleven of the clock in the forenoon, the same day, with force and arms, etc., in the Parish of St. Bennet Grace Church in Bridgeward, London, in the street called Gracechurch Street, unlawfully and tumultuously did assemble and congregate themselves together, to the disturbance of the peace of the said Lord and King....

The reading of the indictment seemed to go on and on. It was obvious to William that the court was trying to charge him and William Mead with anything and everything they could think of. All William had done was lead a prayer meeting on a street corner, but he was being charged with conspiring with William Mead to start a riot. Of course, with his legal training from Lincoln's Inn, he knew why it was important for them to be seen to be causing a riot. It was not enough to be convicted of speaking to a crowd on the street. That was not illegal, although speaking to a crowd and inciting to riot was. In fact the crime carried a stiff jail term if the men were convicted.

"What say you, William Penn and William Mead, are you guilty as you stand indicted, in manner and form as aforesaid, or not guilty?"

Finally the court recorder had finished reading the indictment, and it was time for William to respond. Since the indictment had been so long, William asked if he could first have a written copy of it. "You must first plead to the indictment before you have a copy of it," the court recorder snapped.

William then tried a different tack. He asked the court to promise that he would have a fair hearing on the charges against him and that he would be given ample time to defend against those charges. When he received an assurance that he would be given a fair hearing he said, "Then I plead not guilty in manner and form."

Likewise, William Mead pleaded not guilty, and the court was adjourned. Two days later, on September 3, the court reconvened.

During their arrest William Penn and William Mead had lost their hats. When they entered the courtroom hatless that morning, the lord mayor ordered hats be placed on their heads. When the hats were in place, Thomas Howell, the court recorder, asked William, "Do you know where you are?"

"Yes," William replied.

"Do you not know it is the king's court?"

"I know it to be a court, and I suppose it to be the king's court," William told the recorder.

"Do you not know there is respect due to the court?"

"Yes," William replied.

"Why do you not pay it then?"

"I do so," William said.

"Why do you not pull off your hat, then?" the recorder asked, knowing full well that Quakers refused to doff their hats.

"Because I do not believe that to be any respect," William boldly answered.

"Well, the court sets forty marks apiece upon your heads as a fine for your contempt of the court," the recorder announced.

William was dumbfounded. Forty marks was a lot of money. What angered him more, though, was the fact that despite the court's promise it would grant him a fair hearing, this escapade proved that the court was anything but fair. Finally he exploded, "I desire it might be observed that we came into this court with no hats on, and if they have been put on since, it was by order from the bench; and therefore not we, but the bench, should be fined."

Sir Samuel Starling's face boiled red with anger at William's remark, and he became more enraged when the crowd in the gallery observing the trial cheered William on.

Finally order returned to the courtroom, and the jury were brought in. Once they were seated, three witnesses gave testimony about seeing William Penn speaking on the street corner, though all three testified that they did not hear what he was saying. And one of the witnesses said he could not recall seeing William Mead present at the gathering.

After the witnesses had given their testimony, William inquired as to what law they had been charged under. He hoped it was the Conventicle

Act, which he wanted to directly challenge before the court.

"Upon the common law," the court recorder informed him.

"Where is that common law?" William asked.

The recorder retorted that the body of common law was too big for him to name the specific law at that moment.

"This answer I am sure is very short of my question, for if it be common, it should not be hard to produce," William said.

A snicker went through the gallery at the way he had pointed out the obvious to the court.

"Sir, will you plead to your indictment?" the court recorder snapped.

"Shall I plead to an indictment that hath no foundation in law? If it contain that law you say I have broken, why should you decline to produce that law, since it will be impossible for the jury to determine or agree to bring in their verdict, who have not the law produced by which they should measure the truth of this indictment, and the guilt or contrary of my fact?" William said.

"You are a saucy fellow. Speak to the indictment," the recorder demanded.

William refused to address the specific charges contained in the indictment. Instead he argued with the court recorder, goading him to state the specific law under which he and William Mead were being charged. All the while he hoped they would invoke the Conventicle Act, but he began to suspect that the court was reluctant to charge him under the act and thus hold it up for close public scrutiny.

The debate backward and forward between William and Thomas Howell became more and more heated. William found himself quoting passages from memory from some of the most learned law textbooks. The embarrassment of being lectured on the finer points of the law by William only seemed to infuriate the court recorder more. However, William's actions delighted the gallery. Finally, in utter frustration at the course the trial had taken, Sir Samuel Starling ordered that William be taken to the bail-dock.

As two bailiffs grabbed him, William called to the jury, pointing out the unfairness of the way his trial was being prosecuted and urging them to stand up for liberty and justice for all Englishmen.

Finally William was wrestled into the birdcage-like structure located behind a low wall in the far corner of the Old Bailey courtroom. From there he could not see the proceedings or be seen by the jury or the gallery of onlookers. All he could do was listen as William Mead addressed the court.

"You men of the jury," William Mead began, "here I do now stand to answer an indictment against me, which is a bundle of stuff, full of lies and falsehoods; for therein I am accused that I met with force of arms, unlawfully and tumultuously...I say, I am a peaceable man. Therefore, it is a very proper question William Penn demanded in this case, a hearing of the law on which our indictment is grounded."

William Mead then began to argue with the court recorder until he too was thrown into the bail-dock.

With the two defendants locked away, Thomas Howell gave instructions to the jury to go and deliberate and bring back a verdict of guilty. As he spoke, William scrambled up the bars of the cage he and William Mead were locked in until he could see the jury over the low wall. "You of the jury take notice," he called, "that I have not been heard. Neither can you legally depart the court before I have been fully heard, having at least ten or twelve material points to offer, in order to invalidate the indictment."

"Pull that fellow down! Pull him down!" the recorder ordered.

While the bailiffs tried to pull William down, William Mead took over. "Are these according to the rights and privileges of Englishmen that we should not be heard but turned into the bail-dock for making our defense," he called out.

"Take them away into the hole," the recorder snapped.

William Penn and William Mead were dragged from the courtroom and thrown into the hole, a squalid, low cell at the back of Old Bailey that was not even fit to keep animals in. An hour and a half later, the two defendants were dragged from the hole and brought back into court, where the jury was ready to deliver its verdict. Once the two Williams were led into the dock, the court recorder asked Edward Bushel, the jury foreman, to give the verdict.

"How say you? Is William Penn guilty of the matter wherefore he stands indicted in manner and form, or not guilty?" the recorder asked.

"Guilty of speaking on Gracechurch Street," the foreman replied.

"Is that all?" the lord mayor inquired. "Was it not an unlawful assembly? You mean he was speaking to a tumult of people?"

Again, Edward Bushel told the court that all William Penn was guilty of was speaking on Gracechurch Street, but he was certainly not trying to start a riot.

As chief judge of the case, Sir Samuel Starling refused to accept the verdict and ordered the jury to go and deliberate some more until they brought back the verdict of guilty they had been instructed to deliver by the court in the first place.

This time the jury asked for a pen, ink, and paper. A short while later they returned to the gloomy courtroom at Old Bailey and handed over their written verdict. The paper read: "We the jurors, hereafter named, do find William Penn to be guilty of speaking or preaching to an assembly met together in Gracechurch Street, the 14th of August last, 1670. And that William Mead is not guilty of the said indictment."

Fury rose on the faces of the men behind the bench, while a smile of relief spread across William Penn's and William Mead's faces.

Once again the court refused to accept the verdict. Instead the lord mayor ordered that both the defendants and the jury be taken from the courtroom and locked up in Newgate Prison. One would hope, he suggested, that a night in prison would help the jury come to their senses and return the guilty verdict he wanted to hear.

As William was led from the courtroom, he called to the jury, "You are Englishmen, mind your privilege, give not away your right."

At seven o'clock the next morning, the jury and the defendants were dragged back into court. Once again the jury refused to change their verdict. William was guilty only of speaking on Gracechurch Street; no riot was involved. Once again the court refused to accept the verdict, ordering the jury to reconsider. Each time they did so, the verdict was the same.

William could scarcely believe it. The jury refused to buckle. They saw how unfairly the case had been prosecuted and were making a stand for liberty and justice.

The jury and the judges wrangled back and forth as William called out for the verdict to be accepted. William asked the court how a decision of not guilty could be considered an invalid verdict, when the opposite verdict—guilty—would obviously be considered a valid verdict in the eyes of the court.

Obviously frustrated with the outcome of the whole proceeding and annoyed by William's constant questioning and interrupting, the lord mayor ordered, "Stop his mouth! Jailer, bring fetters and stake him to the ground."

Before the jailer could do this to William, the court adjourned. Once again the defendants and the jury were marched off to Newgate Prison for the night. The following morning they were marched from the prison back to the court.

"How say you? Is William Penn guilty, etc., or not guilty?" the jury were asked once again.

"Not guilty," Edward Bushel replied.

William let out a deep sigh of relief when he heard the verdict. The court had demanded a new verdict, and that is what the jury had given.

Sir Samuel Starling and the other officials of the court sat stunned. They could scarcely believe what the jury had done. Finally the lord mayor regained his composure and addressed the jury.

"I am sorry, gentlemen," the lord mayor said. "You have followed your judgments and opinions rather than the good and wholesome advice that was given you. God keep my life out of your hands, but for this the court fines you forty marks a man, and imprisonment till paid."

The lord mayor of London was fining and sentencing the jury to prison because he didn't like their verdict! William could scarcely believe it. Still, the jury had found him not guilty, and he pressed the point. "I demand my liberty, being freed by the jury," he said.

"No, you are in for your fines," the lord mayor replied.

"What fines?" William asked.

"For contempt of court," Sir Samuel Starling snapped back.

William protested. How could the court fine and imprison him for the obviously trumped-up charge of failing to remove his hat while ignoring the clear finding of the jury that he was not guilty and should be released from custody.

The lord mayor was unmoved. "Take him away. Take him out of the court," he ordered.

Once again bailiffs led the two defendants and the jury back to Newgate Prison, where they were locked up until their fines were paid.

The next day William's father arranged for his and William Mead's fines to be paid. That afternoon the two men walked out of the prison free once again.

Upon his release William set out right away for Wanstead to see his family and learn how his father was.

Chapter 10

A Landmark Decision

During the time he was on trial, William worried about his father's health. His mother had sent notes telling him how ill his father was, and William hurried home to see if his mother had been exaggerating.

As soon as he got home on September 9, 1670, William rushed to his father's bedside. His mother had not exaggerated. His father was gravely ill. Nevertheless Sir William Penn reached out his hand and welcomed his oldest son home. "Sit down," he said. "I have been thinking much and have much to tell you."

William pulled up a chair and sat looking into his father's eyes. Immediately he noticed there was something different about them. Gone were all the anger and pride, and in their place was a gentle-ness William had not seen before.

"Son William, I am weary of the world. I would not live over my days again, if I could command them with a wish, for the snares of life are greater than the fears of death.... Let nothing in this world tempt you to wrong your conscience. I charge you, do nothing against your conscience. So will you keep peace at home, which will be a feast to you in a day of trouble."

William held his father's hand and let the tears stream down his face. Finally his father under-stood! He raised his eyes and thanked God that they had both lived long enough to be reconciled.

As it turned out, Sir William Penn had only six more days to live. In that time he wrote to his friend the duke of York. The duke, as the brother of King Charles II, was next in line of succession to the British Crown, since Charles had no sons by his wife. Admiral Penn asked the duke of York to watch over William and try to smooth out any future trouble he might get himself into. A warm letter came straight back from the duke assuring the admiral that the royal brothers would always honor his son, just as they had him.

After the reply arrived, William noticed that his father's health began to fade rapidly. A doctor bled him several times, but it did not seem to help. Sir William Penn spoke one last time to his son. "If you and your friends keep to your plain way of preach-ing, and keep to your plain way of living, you will make an end of the priests to the end of the world.

Bury me by my mother. Live all in love. Shun all manner of evil. And I pray God will bless you all; and He will bless you."

Sir William Penn died on September 16, 1670, and after an elaborate state funeral for England's naval hero, his will was read. He had not cut William off from his inheritance after all, as he had threatened. In fact, William inherited all of his father's land holdings. His mother had the right to live in the family home at Wanstead for as long as she lived, and she, along with Richard and Margaret, got money, jewelry, and silver.

Suddenly William Penn was a very rich man in his own right, not just the son of a rich man. Though William did not have a lot of time right then to think about all the implications of this for him, he was busy following the case of the remaining four jurors from his trial, who had refused to pay their fines to get out of Newgate Prison.

Soon after Sir William Penn's death, the remaining four jurors were released from jail. Immediately they turned around and sued the judge and the court recorder for false arrest. Given the way Sir Samuel Starling had made such a fool of himself during the trial, no judge in London wanted to take the case. Eventually it found its way to the lord chief justice of England, who gathered together eleven other high court judges to review the case. Their decision was unanimous. Juries must be free to render the verdict they think is just and cannot be punished for rendering such a verdict. As the lord chief justice wrote in his opinion, "[a judge] may try to open the eyes of the jurors, but not lead them by the nose."

William, along with many other people in England, hailed the justices' decision. A mean or vindictive judge, as Sir Samuel Starling had been, no longer had the power to force a jury to reach a verdict that went against their conscience or the evidence presented. It was a landmark victory for justice. Of course Sir Samuel Starling was not at all happy about the outcome. The high court's decision had publicly embarrassed him, and he looked for a way to get back at William.

In early February 1671, five months after his father's death, William found himself once again in prison. Sir Samuel Starling had sent police spies to watch his every move, and eventually William was caught preaching in a Quaker home in London and sentenced to six months in Newgate Prison.

Unlike when he was detained in the Tower of London, this time William was not locked up in a cell. Instead he was thrown in with the rest of the prison populace, which ran the gamut from men like him, imprisoned for their religious beliefs, to men who were robbers and murderers. During the day the prisoners were free to walk about in a huge hall, and at night they were locked into a large square room. A massive oak pole stood in the center of the room, and the prisoners stretched their hammocks between it and the wall. So many prisoners were in the room that the hammocks were stacked up three tiers high, while the sick slept on straw on the floor.

Despite the overcrowded conditions, there was some good news. This time William knew exactly how long he was going to be in prison. And other Quakers were locked up in the jail to keep him company.

To help pass the time, William set to work writing. He called the first tract he wrote in Newgate Prison *The Great Case for Liberty of Conscience.* In the tract he argued that a person could be free only if he or she had choices to make, and when those choices were made for a person by someone over him or her, everyone loses out. People must be allowed to test the truth of their beliefs for themselves and see if that was what they really believed or merely what they had been made to believe.

On August 3, 1671, William was released from Newgate Prison and immediately set out to visit Guli Springett. The two had a lot to talk about and not much time to do it in, since William had a new mission to attend to. While in Newgate Prison he had spent a lot of time with fellow Quaker Thomas Rudyard. As soon as they were released, the two men had promised each other they would go to Europe together and speak at Quaker gatherings there.

William and Thomas set sail for Rotterdam in mid-August, soon after George Fox, founder of the Quakers, had set out from England for the New World. During the six months they were gone, William and Thomas preached in a number of Quaker meetings in Holland and Germany. And while he was away, William made a decision—it was time he had a wife. Soon after his return in February 1672, William Penn and Guli Springett announced their intention to be married.

The wedding took place on April 4, 1672, in a small house in Chorleywood called King John's Farm. It was a very plain service, like everything the Quakers did. William and Guli sat side-by-side in the low-ceilinged meeting room, surrounded by other Quakers. After several minutes of sitting in silence, William and Guli stood up, held hands, and in simple English pledged themselves to each other. There were no rings exchanged, no oaths, no flowers, and no best man or bridesmaids. After they had pledged themselves to each other, William and Guli sat down, and the room once again fell into silence. After a while people began to stand and offer prayers for the newlyweds or to share words of encouragement with them. At the end of the service, the marriage license was signed by all present, and the wedding was over.

After the wedding William and Guli moved into a house of their own located in the village of Rickmansworth on the outskirts of London, where life fell into an easy pattern. For the first time in many years William felt able to relax. Despite having to oversee all the land his father had left him, he had a wife he loved and more tracts to write. He also had something else to look forward to—a new baby. Soon after they were married, Guli had become pregnant.

Things were also beginning to improve for the Quakers and other nonconformists. King Charles II had joined France in declaring war on Holland. Because he did not want trouble at home as well as abroad, the king issued the Declaration of Indulgence, which suspended all laws relating to Quakers, Catholics, and other nonconformists. The prison gates of England were swung open, and about five hundred nonconformists were set free. Among them were many of William's Quaker friends and the dissenter John Bunyan, who emerged from prison with a manuscript he had written there entitled *Pilgrim's Progress*.

On a cold, blustery day in January 1673, Gulielma Maria Penn was born. She was a sickly child from the start and, despite the best care available, died seven weeks later. William and Guli were heartbroken.

Two months later more sad news arrived. William's young brother Richard had died suddenly. He was eighteen years old, and William rushed to Wanstead to comfort his mother.

Later that year George Fox returned from America, and William and Guli traveled to Bristol to meet him. It was an encouraging time as he told them how Quaker meetings were flourishing up and down the Atlantic coast of America. Quakers were even meeting together as far away as Barbados.

George Fox arrived back in England just in time for a new wave of persecution. The king needed money for the war against Holland, but Parliament refused to give him any until he took back his Declaration of Indulgence. It was a bitter pill for the king to swallow, but he had little choice.

Parliament also insisted on a new law called the Test Act. Just as the name implied, this law was meant to test a citizen's allegiance to the Church of England and the king. To do this, anyone who wished to hold public office in England had to swear an oath to the king and take communion in the Church of England.

The act sent ripples through the country. Even the king's brother James, the duke of York, had to resign from his post at the Admiralty because he would not join the Church of England. It was the Quakers, however, who once again bore the brunt of the new law. This was because Quakers did not believe that anyone should take an oath. They held steadfast to a verse in the New Testament in which Jesus told His disciples not to swear by any oath but to simply say yes or no. As if that weren't enough, there was no way the Quakers were going to take communion in the Church of England.

Once again dissenters were rounded up for holding meetings in their homes, and in December George Fox and several other leading Quakers were arrested. The imprisoned Quakers found themselves in a serious situation because the Test Act made them guilty of treason against the king and treason was punishable by death.

Many dissenters rallied to try to help those who had been arrested, and eventually all eyes turned toward William Penn. William was a man with many contacts in the royal court. If anyone could appeal for justice, it was William. Guli was heavily pregnant with their second child when William was asked to intervene on behalf of the imprisoned dissenters. He left Guli at home and went straight to London to see what he could do.

In early January 1674 William was granted an audience with James, the duke of York. It was the first time in six years he had been to the royal court, and it felt strange to him to step back into the lavish world of velvet, lace, and exaggerated manners. However, as soon as William saw the duke again, all the strangeness he felt evaporated. James was delighted to be reunited with Sir William Penn's son. He told William that he hadn't forgotten the promise to help William in any way he could. The two men had a long conversation about the way dissenters were being unfairly treated. James was very sympathetic to the problem. After all, as he pointed out, he had been a victim of the Test Act, too.

William stayed in London long enough after the meeting to give George Fox a hopeful report. He then rode back to Rickmansworth to be with Guli. The following month, not one but two babies arrived. The couple named the twins William and Mary. Regrettably, little William was no more robust than baby Gulielma had been, and within a few weeks he died.

The new parents then poured all of their effort into keeping Mary healthy. As they did so, Mary began to grow. William stayed near his home most of the time to be with his wife and new daughter, but he kept a watchful eye on George Fox's case. The courts treated the case like a game, batting it back and forth between a local court and the king's court. Over the next year William became increasingly frustrated in his efforts to help George. While the duke of York had remained true to his word and done all he could to help, it wasn't enough. William began to wonder whether he and his Quaker friends would ever be left in peace to practice their gentle religion.

In the midst of all the legal wrangling over George Fox's case, Guli gave birth to another baby, a boy. They named him Springett, Guli's family name. He was a strong and healthy boy from the start, and his parents were happy to see him thrive, though at the same time eleven-month-old Mary was ill. She died in February 1675, a month after Springett was born.

Once again William and Guli tried to accept God's will for their family and continued on with their lives. They moved from Rickmansworth to a house Guli inherited in Worminghurst Parish, Sussex, about fifteen miles from Brighton. The move was partly to save money. Philip Ford, William's business manager, had advised William that his cash reserves were starting to run low. William was spending most of his time and energy working for the Quaker cause, and he seldom got paid for what he did.

On July 22, 1677, William said good-bye to his wife and son and once again set out for London on his way to Holland. This time he was gone for seven months. While away he was encouraged by the freer way that Dutch and German dissenters were allowed to worship. This gave him hope for Britain. His hopes were dashed, though, when he set foot back on English soil.

A whole new round of persecution was under way, started by the rumor that a plot had been hatched by Catholic priests to conquer England with the help of French and Irish Catholics. King Charles II hastily married his nine-year-old niece Mary, the daughter of the duke of York, to William of Orange. William was a prince of the House of Orange, the Protestant rulers of Holland, and King Charles hoped to assure Parliament that he wanted Protestant marriages in his family and not Catholic ones.

The plan hardly worked. The country was soon rife with anti-Catholic witch-hunts, magistrates were murdered, and mobs attacked innocent people. It all made William sick, and when he dared suggest to Parliament that no one, not even Catholics, should be whipped for their faith, he was branded a "Pope-lover."

In the midst of this hellish inquisition, the Penns had two more children. Letitia was born in March 1678 and William in March two years later. Thankfully both children grew strong and healthy.

As Springett Penn turned five, William worried about him and all the children of Quakers and other dissenters. What kind of future would they have? For all of William's efforts over the years, little had changed in England. Laws, particularly those relating to religion, were constantly changing and were used as an excuse to take money and freedom from anyone Parliament disagreed with. But deep within William a plan was beginning to stir. There had to be a place to get away to—a place that would be ruled by laws and not rulers, where every man, woman, and child had the right to follow his or her conscience in matters of religion, and where tolerance prevailed. There was no land in England or Ireland where such an experiment could be tried, but one place on earth did have vast tracts of sparsely settled land—America!

Chapter 11

A Holy Experiment

William Penn petitioned the king for a tract of land between Maryland and New Jersey. The same day that the king received the petition he approved it and sent word to his Privy Council to begin the paperwork needed to make the land grant lawful.

The speed at which the grant was approved and the amount of land that King Charles II offered in the grant staggered not only William but also everyone else involved with the transfer. The land was estimated to be about 45,000 square miles, though it was impossible to know for sure, since no one had been inland far enough to survey the exact location of the western boundary. As a result, the actual area of the land grant could be even bigger than it was estimated to be. All this

land made William Penn the largest private landowner in the world.

In return for a payment of two beaver pelts a
year, the king gave William absolute power over his
new land. William could divide the land into counties and towns and set up a system of laws. The
only thing he could not do was to create a private
army to wage war. For the peace-loving William,
that was not a restriction at all.

Many people tried to imagine why King Charles
II had been so generous. Although he technically
owed William eleven thousand pounds, money that
Admiral Penn had "loaned" him, such loans were
never paid back. They were looked upon as payment for certain privileges from the king. So all
sorts of theories developed to explain the king's
generosity. Perhaps he was about to crack down
even harder on dissenters and wanted William
Penn out of harm's way so that he would not be
hung. Or perhaps King Charles was preparing a
large colony to which he could deport those people
who refused to yield to the Church of England.
Maybe he was just tired of having the Quakers
around making a fuss all the time about the rights
of Englishmen. No one knew what the king's
motives were in making such a large land grant.
William certainly did not know, and he didn't ask!
Instead he accepted the land grant as God's gift to
all dissenters.

The first thing this new territory in America
needed was a name. William liked Sylvania, which
meant the forest, but King Charles wanted the
name Penn added to the front of it. This did not sit

well with William. The Quakers were modest, humble people. The last thing a Quaker like William wanted was to have a colony named after him.

But the king was insistent. "Not after you," he told William. "I propose you name the colony Pennsylvania after your father, Sir William Penn."

William could hardly argue with the idea of honoring his father, and so the name of the new territory became Pennsylvania.

On March 4, 1681, King Charles II signed the charter for the new colony, and then it was certified and deposited in the office of the Lord Chancellor. It was official. Thirty-six-year-old William Penn was the sole proprietor of all of Pennsylvania, to do with it as he liked.

The following day William wrote a letter to Robert Turner, an old Quaker friend. He ended the letter by saying, "It is a clear and just thing, and my God that has given it to me through many difficulties, will, I believe, bless it and make it the seed of a nation. I shall have a tender care to the government, that it be well laid at first."

The next letter William wrote he had to think about for a long time because it was important he convey the right message. The letter was to the thousand or so Swedish, Dutch, and English people who had already settled in Pennsylvania. He wanted them to feel safe and confident about their future. He wrote:

> My Friends, I hope you will not be troubled with your change. You are now fixed at the mercy of no governor that comes to

make his fortune great. You shall be governed by laws of your own making, and live a free, and if you will, a sober and industrious people. I shall not usurp the right of any or oppress his person...God has furnished me with a better resolution and has given me the grace to keep it.

William wrote one more important letter. This time he wrote to the people who had lived on the land for thousands of years—the Indians. "My Friends," William started the letter, "there is one great God and power that hath made the world and all things therein, to whom you and I, and all people owe their being and well-being, and to whom you and I must one day give an account for all that we have done in the world." He explained to them how the King of England had given him the land they now lived on, and then he wrote:

But I desire to enjoy it with your love and consent, that we may always live together as neighbors and friends, else what would the great God say to us, who hath made us not to devour and destroy one another, but to live soberly and kindly together in the world?...I am very sensible of the unkindness and injustice that hath been too much exercised toward you by the people of these parts of the world, who have sought to make great advantages by you, rather than be examples of justice and goodness unto you.... But I am not such a man, as is well known in my own country, I have great love and regard for you, and desire to gain your love and friendship by a kind, just and peaceable life; and the people I send are of the same mind...I shall shortly come to see you myself, at which time we may more largely and freely confer...I am, your loving friend, William Penn.

Of course the letters had to be delivered to the citizens and the Indians, and William chose his cousin, William Markham, to take them to Pennsylvania. He made William his deputy governor and, along with having him deliver the letters, ordered him to settle boundary arguments, open courts, and appoint sheriffs and justices of the peace.

William Markham left on the first available ship, and once he was on his way, William set about the task of attracting individuals and families to his new land in America. He called these people First Adventurers. Although William had never been to America, he needed to write a tract telling English people what they could expect if they emigrated there. This presented a problem, and William set about interviewing anyone he could think of who could help him describe the landscape and conditions in America. He interviewed sea captains, preachers, royal officials, traders, and others with land holdings in America. Once he had gathered all the information he could from them, he began writing a tract he called *A Brief Account of the Province of Pennsylvania.*

The next tract he wrote was entitled *Certain Conditions and Concessions Agreed Upon by William Penn, Proprietary and Governor of the Province of Pennsylvania.* In this tract he listed twenty points. The first ten points dealt with exactly how the land was to be laid out for sale. Large plots were to be set aside for towns and cities, and every purchaser of farmland would be given ten acres of land in the city for every five hundred acres that he bought or rented in the country. And having acquired the land, every farmer had three years to plant something on it. All land distributed in Pennsylvania would be subject to a small tax called a quitrent, which was payable to William Penn personally. Quitrents were the usual way in which the proprietor of a province made enough money to keep the government going and in most cases make a profit for himself, though as William had pointed out to the existing settlers, he had no plans to grow rich off the land.

The next five points William dealt with in the tract were about how the Indians living in Pennsylvania should be dealt with. Since William wanted them to have the same rights as everyone else, he wrote that all trade with Indians should be carried out in public markets and in a fair manner. If an Indian was accused of a crime, he was to be tried before a judge and jury consisting of six settlers and six Indians.

The last five points outlined laws regarding such things as branding livestock, registering ships, and collecting debts.

William also wrote the preface for the *Charter of Liberties,* a legal document that would guide the establishment of a system of government and laws in his new colony. In the preface he summed up his beliefs regarding government and laws.

> Governments, like clocks, go from the motion men give them; and as governments are made and moved by men, so by them are they ruined too.... Let me be good, and the government cannot be bad; if it be ill, they [the people] will cure it.... We have...to the best of our skill, contrived and composed the Frame and Laws of this government...to support power in reverence to the people, and to secure people from the abuse of power.... Liberty without obedience is confusion, and obedience without liberty is slavery.

The *Charter of Liberties* was signed by fifteen of the First Adventurers who were preparing to leave for Pennsylvania. According to the charter, in an election in which every freeman or landowner could vote, a council and an assembly would be chosen to govern the colony. As well in the colony there would be freedom of religion, trials by jury, and no death penalty except for treason and murder.

Now that William had his thoughts on paper, he traveled around England encouraging Quakers to join his new community, which he called a Holy Experiment. He paid all the printing and traveling expenses out of his own pocket, and he soon began to see that Pennsylvania would cost him a lot more money before he ever saw a profit from the land.

As he was coming to this realization, an English trading company made William a stunning offer. It would pay him six thousand pounds in exchange for the rights to be the only company that traded furs with the Indians. The money would have been welcome, but William did not consider the offer for a moment. In his letter to the Indians, he had promised that his colonists would be examples of justice and goodness to them. That included protecting the Indians from trading companies that might take advantage of them.

To protect the Indians, William realized that he had to set up an official trading network. He encouraged a group of soon-to-be settlers to form the Free Society of Traders. He gave the society twenty thousand acres of land to get started and charged them with dealing with the Indians in a fair and open manner.

While William was writing the preface to the *Charter of Liberties*, he received word that his mother had died, and so he went to Wanstead to make the funeral arrangements.

In early October 1681 William and Guli stood on the London docks and waved good-bye to the first party of settlers setting sail for Pennsylvania aboard the *John and Sarah*. Their passage had cost six pounds for each adult, fifty shillings for those under ten, and nothing for babies. Each adult passenger was allowed to take one chest with him or her on the boat. Any other freight was charged at a rate of forty shillings a ton.

It was exciting to see the ship slip its mooring and move off downriver. Those aboard included three land commissioners William had appointed. Their job was to assign lots, lay out roads, and find a suitable site for a capital city for the colony. William would like to have been aboard ship with them all, but since there was so much work still to do in London, he had decided to travel to Pennsylvania later. That way more settlers would have arrived there who could help him set up the new government and lay out the new towns and cities.

Finally, eleven months later, it was William's turn to set sail. The *Welcome*, the ship that would carry him to his new colony, was to leave from Deal on the southeast coast of England. Guli accompanied him part of the way there before having to turn around and head back home to look after the children. She had decided to stay in England for a while, since her mother had just died and she was expecting another baby. Before they parted, Guli gave William a blue silk sash with tassels on it that she had sewn. "Wear it on special occasions," she said, "and remember me until we meet again."

Philip Ford, William's trusted business manager of thirteen years, and his wife, Bridget, accompanied William the rest of the way to the ship. Shortly before departing, Philip handed over three documents for William to sign. He assured William they were routine contracts that needed his signature. William was too caught up in the excitement of leaving to read them all, so he signed the papers and handed them back to Philip.

The *Welcome* waited packed and ready for two days for enough wind to fill her sails. Finally, on August 30, 1682, the ship weighed anchor and began making her way to America. Sails billowed from all three masts, and William and the nearly one hundred other Quakers aboard stood on deck and watched as England faded from view. Three thousand miles of unpredictable ocean now lay between them and their destination.

While the *Welcome* was 108 feet long and weighed 248 tons, it was anything but sleek in the water. It bobbed up and down and moved from side to side. And instead of cutting through the waves, it rode up and over them. Soon the motion of the ship had many of the passengers below deck vomiting or stretched out on their straw mattresses.

Several days out from Deal, disaster struck the *Welcome*. Several of the passengers came down with smallpox, which quickly spread. Since he had contracted smallpox when he was three, William was immune to the ravages of the disease, and he quickly began to help those who were sick. In the darkness below deck, where no candle or lamp could be lit for fear it might set the ship ablaze, he did what he could. He tried to keep those feverishly hot from the disease cool by bathing them. However, since they were in the middle of the Atlantic Ocean, all the fresh water aboard was needed for drinking, watering the livestock, and cooking. So William was forced to use salt water to bathe people. Although the water of the North Atlantic was plenty cold, the salt stung the open sores that erupted on the skin of those infected with the disease.

Finally, after many days, the smallpox outbreak began to subside, but not before it had killed thirty-one people, nearly one-third of the new settlers aboard. William held funeral services for the dead, who were buried at sea, and tried to comfort and encourage those who had lost loved ones.

Slowly the *Welcome* creaked and groaned its way forward until finally, on the fifty-third day of the voyage, the squawking of gulls brought William out onto the poop deck of the ship. He looked up and watched as the birds soared around the sails. And as he watched, his spirit soared, too. The presence of the birds could mean only one thing— they were getting close to land. Somewhere, not far over the horizon, was America.

One and one-half days later, a long gray-brown streak appeared faint on the horizon. "The Capes of Delaware," the captain announced.

William stood transfixed and watched as the streak on the horizon grew to become a landform covered with lush forest. The cape continued to grow as the ship moved closer, until the *Welcome* slipped around it and into a wide bay.

"I can hardly believe it. Look how beautiful this place is, and feel how warm," said one of the Quaker men standing nearby.

William nodded gently. It was indeed a beautiful sight, and the man was right. By now in England a person would need a heavy cape to keep warm when venturing outdoors, but William had on only a vest and jacket and did not feel cold at all.

William had heard so much about the land from people who had been there. He had read about it, dreamed about it, but now he was seeing it with his own eyes. He drank in the view as the *Welcome* crossed the bay and began to make her way up the Delaware River.

As they moved upriver, William reminded himself that it wasn't simply the beauty of the landscape or the pleasant weather that had brought him across the Atlantic Ocean. What had brought him was the new kind of community he planned to establish on this land. He was determined to have a community based upon the steadfast rule of law and not on the whim of kings and tyrants. It would be a tolerant community that did not worry itself with other people's faith or ethnic background. Above all, it would be a community where justice and liberty were the norm for every person. It was a Holy Experiment, and if he was successful, Pennsylvania would be a very different place than England, or anywhere else in the world for that matter.

On October 27, 1682, after fifty-eight days at sea, the *Welcome* dropped anchor off the town of New Castle. Those aboard had paid a high price for the voyage. Many were now widows, widowers, or orphans as a result of the smallpox outbreak.

The Dutch had built New Castle, and William quickly recognized their influence in the design of the dozen or so brick houses with high-pitched roofs that made up the town. Indeed, the town reminded him of several of the small villages he had visited and spoken in on his trips to Holland. A small fort was perched right on the edge of the river in front of the town, and next to it was a weigh-house where captains and traders could weigh their cargoes. Around the town a swath of land several hundred feet wide had been cleared from the forest. Several cows grazed on the lush grass that now grew there. And beyond the town and the meadow, the forest was still ablaze in the glory of its fall colors.

Along the riverbank beside the town, a crowd had gathered to welcome William. He could see William Markham and Thomas Holme, the official surveyor whose job it was to mark the boundaries of the new colony. Among the crowd he could see Indians, who were nearly naked and whose dark copper skin gleamed in the late afternoon sun. William could scarcely wait to go ashore. But he would have to be patient. By the time the *Welcome* was firmly at anchor and her sails furled, darkness was beginning to fall, and it was too late to bring out boats to ferry William and the other passengers ashore. William would have to wait until morning before he finally set his feet on the New World.

Chapter 12

First Steps
on American Soil

William was awakened early the next morning by the sound of voices coming from all around the ship. He stumbled through the darkness of his unlit cabin up on deck. Shielding his eyes against the bright morning sun that climbed above the eastern horizon he gazed out at the river. All around the *Welcome* were people in boats and barges beckoning their new governor ashore. William even noticed a number of Indians paddling in their dugout canoes among the boats.

William went below, collected his pouch of documents, put on the blue sash Guli had given him, and climbed down into one of the boats. He was then ferried ashore, where he took his first steps on American soil. He warmly greeted William Markham and Thomas Holme and was then introduced to

John Moll and Ephraim Harman, attorneys for the king. William, as proprietor of the new colony, was presented with the key to the fort, and then John Moll gave him a clod of earth with a twig stuck in it. This was a symbolic gift meant to represent the land William was taking possession of.

Following the presentation of these gifts, a table and chair were brought out and placed on the grass beside the river, where the formal transfer of the land to William Penn was carried out. Both William and the king's two attorneys signed the document, surrendering authority for the land to William. William Markham and Thomas Holme signed it as witnesses. Upon the signatures being affixed to the document, Pennsylvania was born. With the official signing over of the land complete, a representative from the Swedes living in the new colony stepped forward and pledged their support to William.

Later in the day William returned to the *Welcome*. New Castle was not his final destination. The settlement of Upland, farther up the Delaware River, was where he would leave the ship.

In Upland William stayed at the home of Robert Wade and attended a Quaker meeting. He was eager, however, to inspect the site Thomas had selected as a possible place for a capital city, farther upstream beyond where the Schuylkill River flowed into the Delaware. A small trading post called Coaquannock by the local Lenni Lenape Indians already existed at the site. As the barge carrying William moved upstream, the banks of the Delaware rose high, with a sandy beach at the base. This pleased William greatly, as he had instructed his surveyor to look for a spot for the city that would not flood easily.

Suddenly William saw canoes being pushed out from the riverbank. The boats were filled with Indian men. Their heads were shaved except for a topknot held in place by a single feather, and their muscular bodies were smeared with bear fat. The men paddled around William's barge looking solemn. William nodded to them and allowed them to study him before they paddled away.

Word that William Penn was coming had already reached the inhabitants of Coaquannock. The people stood on the bank of the river to greet him. William made a short speech, and then the residents proudly showed him around their village. The village comprised ten houses set in a row, with the Blue Anchor tavern located at one end. The tavern, which also served as the post office and trading post, was the oldest building in town, having been built ten years before.

William walked all over the site for his proposed city. It was perfect. For a distance the Schuylkill River flowed parallel to the Delaware before emptying into the larger river south of the proposed site. This left a long finger of land about two miles wide between the two navigable rivers, ideal for William's city. The land was dry and fertile, and there was plenty of clay from which bricks could be made. As well there were plenty of stones that could be used for building.

Satisfied that this was the site, William pulled out the proposed plan for his new city. The plan called for straight, wide streets, unlike the narrow, crowded streets of London. A street one hundred feet wide would run between the Delaware and the Schuylkill Rivers, and another street of equal width would divide the town north to south. Where the two streets crossed would be a ten-acre public square. Still mindful of the great fire of London, William decided that each house should stand alone on its own lawn, thereby reducing the fire hazard.

The proposed city had a name too. William had thought long and hard about it. He didn't want to name it after a person or place like virtually every other city in the New World. Instead he named it after the way he hoped the citizens of the new city would treat one another. He called it Philadelphia, which meant brotherly love. The name came from combining two Greek words, *philos* (love) and *adelphos* (brother).

After viewing the proposed site for Philadelphia, William ordered that work begin on the new city right away.

From the site of the new city, William traveled twenty-four miles on up the Delaware River. His cousin had purchased a site there for William's new home. William already knew that he wanted to name the place Pennsbury, and once again he was pleased with the choice of site, which sat beside a crook in the river. The land had cost William two thousand feet of wampum, three hundred Dutch gilders, and twenty blankets, along with an assortment of guns, hoes, coats, and stockings. That William was prepared to pay for the land at all showed the Indians that he meant what he had written in his letter to them. According to English law, the entire land of Pennsylvania already belonged to William. All he had to do was force the Indians off the land, using any method available to him. But William Penn had a different kind of colony in mind, a place where even native people would be treated fairly. He remembered back to his boyhood days in Ireland, when the British came and took land that did not belong to them. William was determined not to cause the kind of heartache in the Indians that he had seen in the people of Ireland when their land was confiscated.

William had plans for Pennsbury, too, and as he stood on the wooded site, he could almost see the house. It would be a three-story, red-brick house with a high-pitched slate roof. A long, tree-lined path would lead to a boathouse at the river's edge. The Delaware River would be his road to and from Philadelphia. William also imagined flower gardens with English roses and, in time, large walnut trees transplanted from England. And there would also be a brew house, a bake house, and a barn for the horses.

William gave orders for work to begin on Pennsbury, and then he climbed onto the barge for the trip back downriver. As they floated along, William thanked William Markham and Thomas Holme for the fine job they had done in laying the foundations of Pennsylvania. William went to stay with his friend Thomas Fairman, who had a spacious house at Shackamaxon, just north of the site for Philadelphia.

Once work on Philadelphia and his new home was under way, William decided the next thing to do was open a court and begin hearing the various land claims of settlers. With more and more people arriving in the colony, disagreements about the boundaries of parcels of land quickly arose, especially since Pennsylvania had not been fully surveyed.

Even though he had legal training, William tried to stay in the background, advising but not insisting on the way the court proceeded. He was determined that Pennsylvania be ruled by laws and not by a man. In fact, he was so determined that he did something no one had done before. In the legal framework he set up for the colony, he included laws that made it impossible for him to have too much power. He had deliberately put himself under the same laws as everyone else. He also had done something that had never been tried before. He wrote the laws in such a way that they could be changed if the needs of the people changed.

In fact, many Quakers did not like the way William had written some of the laws of Pennsylvania. Several people complained that half the members of the ruling council were from other religious groups. They believed that Quakers should always be the majority in the government so that they could keep control of Pennsylvania. William disagreed. "If you Quakers had it in your power, none should have a part in the government but those of your own way," he said. After living all of his life under a system where religion exerted great control over government, William was not prepared to interfere with his new democracy. Let the settlers vote for whomever they want, Quaker or otherwise, he argued.

Soon after arriving in Pennsylvania, William decided he needed to learn the language of the Delaware Indians, who inhabited the eastern part of the colony. Although he already spoke Greek, French, and Latin fluently, as well as English, William found the new language difficult, but not impossible, to learn.

William's mastery of the language was a great help when he met with the local Indians at Shackamaxon. William rode up to the meeting on a brown stallion. He was dressed in the plain clothes of a Quaker and wore the blue silk sash Guli had made for him that he used to denote his position as governor of Pennsylvania.

The Indians had gathered under a huge elm tree that was said to be three hundred years old. They sat in their customary half circle, with the chief dressed in ceremonial feather headdress and deerskin leggings and seated in the middle.

From the way the Indians looked at him, William could tell they were impressed. And their eyes lit up when he dismounted and addressed them in their language. He told them that he did not trust in rifles and swords but put his trust in faith and goodwill. He and the people who had come to live in Pennsylvania did not want to hurt the Indians but wanted to treat them fairly and be their friends.

When William had finished speaking, the chief stood and declared, "We desire peace and friendship with our white brothers."

And that is what William gave them. He worked hard to develop friendship with the Indians. He visited their camps, ate their food, talked with them by their campfires, and joined in their games. And at thirty-eight, William was probably the fittest white man the Indians had encountered. He could outrun and outwrestle many of the young braves.

Soon after his meeting with the Delaware Indians, William had a meeting with Lord Baltimore, proprietor of Maryland. However, this meeting was not one William looked forward to. A dispute over the border between Pennsylvania and Maryland had erupted as soon as William Markham had arrived in America, and it had not yet been settled. There were two different ways of determining where the boundary lay. In Lord Baltimore's deed to Maryland, the northern border was defined as "south of the 40 degrees of north latitude." In William Penn's deed to Pennsylvania, the boundary was defined as the line "two degrees north from Watkin's Point." To their dismay, the 40 degrees of north latitude in Lord Baltimore's deed was significantly north of the boundary line in William's deed. Thus, both men claimed legal right to the same tract of land. To make matters worse, the new city of Philadelphia, now under construction, fell within the land Lord Baltimore claimed. This misunderstanding occurred because there were few accurate maps of the American colonies and most colonies had not been fully surveyed.

In December 1682 William traveled to Maryland to meet with Lord Baltimore. But instead of solving the disagreement, the visit seemed to make the matter worse. Lord Baltimore also brought up the question of who owned Delaware. In his deed Lord Baltimore had been granted "parts of America not yet cultivated and planted (by white people)." Before he was given his charter, thirty people had been living in a tiny settlement on the edge of Delaware Bay. However, Indians had raided the settlement and killed its inhabitants, and so at the time Lord Baltimore took possession of Maryland no white people were cultivating and planting in Delaware—but they had been, and their crops were still growing! As a result Lord Baltimore thought Delaware should belong to him. But shortly before William had left England, the duke of York had given him title to the three counties that the land comprised between Delaware Bay and Chesapeake Bay.

The situation over the ownership of Delaware only inflamed the disagreement between William and Lord Baltimore. At the meeting both men stood their ground and nothing was resolved. However, they agreed to meet again later to discuss the situation. Indeed, the agreement to keep talking seemed to be the only good thing to come out of the meeting. William believed that if they kept talking, they would eventually reach an agreement

over the issue without having to take the disagreement across the Atlantic to England, where it could
take years to resolve in court.

Meanwhile, ships filled with settlers kept arriving in Pennsylvania. They came from England,
Wales, Ireland, and areas of Holland and Germany
that William had visited on his missionary travels
to Europe. One of the ships also brought a letter
containing sad news. Guli had given birth to a girl
in early March 1683, but the child had lived only
three weeks, leaving Guli weak and depressed.
William wished he could be with her, but setting
up the government, settling land claims, and over-
seeing the building of Philadelphia as well as his
home at Pennsbury took all of his time. He felt
sure that if he left Pennsylvania right then, all he
had worked so hard to accomplish would fall apart.

William ended up leaving Pennsylvania sooner
than he wanted, however. He had suggested several
compromises to resolve the boundary issue, but
Lord Baltimore had rejected all of them. Instead
Lord Baltimore began a writing campaign back to
England, seeking to gather support to oust William
from Pennsylvania. Then he decided to go in person
and speak with the king. This left William with little
choice but to follow Lord Baltimore to London. If he
wanted to save Philadelphia, he would have to seek
favor at the royal court, where he hoped the duke
of York was still his ally.

Before he boarded the *Endeavor* for the trip
back to England, William wrote a letter to the men
he had left in charge of his Holy Experiment. Along

with the letter he wrote a prayer of encouragement for the colony.

> My love and my life is to you, and with you; and no water can quench it, nor distance wear it out, or bring it to an end. I have been with you, cared over you and served you with unfeigned love; and you are beloved of me, and near to me, beyond utterance.

As William sailed away in August 1684, he thought of all that had been achieved in the nearly two years since he had arrived in Pennsylvania. Over fifty ships had arrived with settlers. The population of Pennsylvania now stood at about seven thousand. The city of Philadelphia had grown to a bustling town of twenty-five hundred people living in 350 houses, many of them made of brick. Twenty smaller towns had sprung up in the colony, creating new industries. Farmers were raising crops and healthy livestock on the fertile plains, and ships were ferrying produce back to England. The Indian tribes were growing prosperous, too, selling a variety of furs such as panther, fox, mink, wildcat, muskrat, and wolf to the Free Society of Traders. Everything was going better than William expected, and he had great hope that it would continue to do so if he could settle the dispute with Lord Baltimore.

As the *Endeavor* pitched and rolled its way eastward across the Atlantic, William hoped that it wouldn't be too long before he was back in Pennsylvania.

Chapter 13

Caught in the Middle

William arrived back home in Worminghurst just in time for his fortieth birthday. He was relieved to finally be there and find that Guli and the three children were well. Nine-year-old Springett was the only one of the children to remember his father, though six-year-old Letitia and four-year-old William Jr. soon lost their shyness around him.

For the first few days, William hardly left the house. He had so much to talk about with Guli. They planned to return to Pennsylvania with the children as soon as the dispute over the border with Maryland was resolved. William thought this would take a few months at most. If he had known the trials that lay ahead for him, he would not have spent his time writing letters of instruction to the manager at Pennsbury. In the letters he urged his manager to employ carpenters to build the kitchen, two larders, a washhouse, and an ironing room in preparation for the entire family's return. William even dispatched a gardener from England to plant and tend the gardens he imagined surrounding his new home.

As soon as he was rested and reacquainted with his family, William set out for London to seek an audience with the king and the duke of York. He found them both looking sickly and, worse, more worried about dissenters than ever. King Charles II was ruling with a heavy hand. He had disbanded Parliament, and the punishment against anyone who did not agree with him was swift and cruel.

The more William learned about the new wave of persecution going on, the more he despaired that England would ever be a country based on laws, and the more he saw how important Pennsylvania was as a refuge from the madness of religious persecution.

The king told William that he would allow the Privy Council to hear the Penn-Baltimore case, but William soon discovered that his aide had forgotten to pack vital paperwork for the hearing, and so he had to ask for a delay. The delay upset William greatly, and he wrote back to Pennsylvania to have the paperwork forwarded to him on the first available ship. In the meantime he decided to make the best of a bad situation. He passed his time working for the release of nearly fifteen hundred Quakers who had been imprisoned as a result of the harsh new edicts of King Charles. William worked especially hard to help Richard Vickris, a

Bristol merchant who was under a death sentence because he would not take an oath.

Pardoning Richard Vickris was one of the last official acts King Charles II performed. On February 1, 1685, while his barber shaved him, the king collapsed. Fearing that Prince William of Orange or the king's illegitimate son James Scott, the duke of Monmouth, might use the opportunity to seize the British Crown and place the country firmly back under Protestant rule, the duke of York immediately ordered all ports closed. Guards were posted everywhere in London.

Despite the best medical care of the day, King Charles grew sicker. His twelve physicians bled him, placed red-hot frying pans near his head and the soles of his feet, and fed him crushed stones from the stomach of a goat mixed with black cherry water. These "cures" notwithstanding, five days later, on February 6, the king died. Church bells rang out all over England, and huge bonfires lit up the night sky. The king's brother James, the duke of York, was declared his successor.

At first William was hopeful that King James II would ease the persecution of dissenters. After all, the new king was a Catholic, and Catholics had also borne the brunt of the Church of England's persecution. William's optimism was encouraged when in a private meeting King James told him that he desired "all peaceable people to be left alone to practice whatever religion they chose."

Regrettably the king's words were kinder than his deeds. King James set in motion a slow but steady plan to return England to the Catholic fold.

Protestants were outraged, and in June the duke of Monmouth returned from exile in Holland to lead an attack on his uncle and take his father's place on the English throne. He and his followers landed in Dorset and got as far as Sedgemoor, where King James's troops stopped their advance in a vicious attack known as the Bloody Assize. The duke of Monmouth was captured in the battle, and King James II had him beheaded in London soon afterward.

The sudden change of monarch and the unrest that went with it left William Penn in a difficult position. He was a personal friend of King James. Before his death, Sir William Penn had asked James to look after his son. But now William did not agree with what the king was doing, and as he thought about it, he decided he had two choices. He could side with those who were agitating for more religious freedom and make the king angry, or he could continue to try to work with the king and help him take less extreme measures against dissenters. In the end, one thing above all else guided William in his choice. He felt he had to do whatever it took to get the boundary dispute between Pennsylvania and Maryland settled so that he could return to America as soon as possible. As a result he decided the best way to get the dispute resolved quickly was to stay close to King James. Whatever else happened, as long as Pennsylvania existed, dissenters would have a safe haven in an unstable world.

The world seemed to be becoming more unstable each day. In France King Louis XIV, a Catholic, was terrorizing Huguenot Protestants. They had been able to live and work freely under a law called the Edict of Nantes, but now King Louis had announced he was revoking the edict. Protestants were forbidden to travel, and soldiers were assigned quarters in their homes with instructions to treat them harshly until they converted to the Catholic faith. Tens of thousands of Huguenot Protestants fled to England, risking death if they were caught. In the south of France entire cities were abandoned.

William saw the same clampdown on religious freedom happening in England. Huge bonfires burned books by men like John Locke, who had written about democratic governments, and John Milton. One of William's good friends, Algernon Sydney, was hanged for writing a manuscript that called for Parliament to be given political power over the monarch. There were other public displays of terror as well. An Anabaptist woman named Elizabeth Gaunt was accused of sheltering a rebel in her home. After a trial that proved to be a mockery of justice, she was sentenced to be burned at the stake. William witnessed the horrible event. The crowd was so moved by Elizabeth Gaunt's calmness that they stood weeping as the fire consumed her.

Soon the problems of the country reached out and touched William. Many people were incensed that he remained friendly with King James, and rumors began to circulate that he had secretly converted to the Catholic faith.

While all of this was going on, William impatiently waited for a hearing date on the boundary dispute to be set. Finally on September 2, 1685, a full year after leaving Pennsylvania, William and Lord Baltimore stood before the Privy Council. William won the first round. The Privy Council announced that the land in Delaware that was in dispute was in fact under cultivation by the Dutch at the time of the establishment of Maryland and so did not fall under Lord Baltimore's land charter. Therefore the land had belonged to the duke of York, and he had been right in granting it to William Penn.

William was very encouraged by this first victory, although he knew there were still more battles ahead. He rushed back to Worminghurst to tell Guli the good news and write a new batch of letters to his manager authorizing more building at Pennsbury. If things continued to go well, he intended to move his family to America in the spring.

While he waited, William tried to do whatever he could to settle the ongoing atmosphere of religious intolerance. He kept reminding the king about his promise that all peaceful men would be able to live their lives freely under his reign. Largely because of this pressure from William, King James II did issue a Declaration of Indulgence granting freedom of worship to both Catholics and dissenters.

On November 17, 1685, Guli gave birth to a new daughter, whom they named Gulielma Maria Penn. Soon after the birth of the baby, King James asked William to go on a peacekeeping mission to

Holland to speak with his daughter Mary, who was the wife of Prince William of Orange, the Protestant leader of Holland. William tried to convince the prince and princess that King James would not attack them, but neither William nor Mary believed him.

When William returned to England, he discovered that the king had created a new disaster for himself. He had tried to appoint Catholic bishops to positions in the Church of England and had brought seven Protestant bishops to trial for refusing to read out his orders in their churches.

William was shocked at how badly things were going. He wondered how the king could make such good promises and then rule so poorly. Still, the land dispute between Pennsylvania and Maryland had not been properly settled, and so William felt he had to stay close to the king. He moved his family into a house two miles from Windsor Castle, where he would be closer to the royal court.

Soon after the move an important event occurred. King James's second wife, the Italian Princess Mary of Modena, gave birth to a son and heir to the throne—a Catholic heir. Until this time most English people expected that when King James II died the throne would pass to Mary, his Protestant daughter from his first marriage. Now, with the arrival of a Catholic Prince of Wales, everything changed.

England was in an uproar. Rumors circulated that the baby was not really a prince at all but an imposter smuggled into the palace in a warming pan. Some people believed that any day Catholics would begin killing Protestants and take over all government positions. In the midst of this chaos, people learned that the leaders of the Church of England and members of Parliament had invited William of Orange, Mary's husband, to invade England and overthrow his father-in-law, King James II. Most people, including King James II, believed that William of Orange was on his way to invade with large numbers of troops. Fearing for his life, the king and his family fled to the safety of King Louis XIV's court in France.

This all happened so fast that William hardly had time to comprehend it. By Christmas 1688 King James II was gone and William and Mary were waiting for an invitation from Parliament to rule as joint sovereigns. Then the Glorious Revolution, as it was called, would be complete.

Meanwhile William and his family soon found themselves in strife. William had been a loyal friend to King James II, trying to steer him and the country toward religious tolerance. Now rumors grew that William had secretly been a Catholic all along and that he was plotting with King Louis of France to return James to the throne of England.

William and Mary became the king and queen of England in January 1689, and they immediately set about championing a bill of rights that gave English people the right to have their own religion once and for all. It was the culmination of what William had worked so hard and so long to achieve, but ironically he was not able to celebrate.

In February a warrant was signed for his arrest upon "suspicion of high treason."

The warrant had been issued because a man named Fuller had sworn that he knew that William was part of a plot to overthrow the new monarchs. It was a vicious lie and a bitter pill to swallow. William decided to go into hiding until things calmed down. He stayed with various friends in London, seeing Guli and the children whenever a secret visit could be arranged. He also wrote a letter to the Quakers in London explaining his reason for going into hiding.

> My privacy is not because men have sworn truly, but falsely against me; "for wicked men have laid in wait for me, and false witnesses have laid to my charge things that I knew not." I have done some good, and would have done more, and hurt no man, but always desired the truth.... Feel me near you, my dear and beloved brethren, and leave me not, nor forsake....

While in hiding William wrote another letter, this time to the residents of Pennsylvania who were busy feuding and arguing among themselves. He scolded them, saying:

> Your division has torn me to pieces and opened those wounds that malice gave me here, and time and patience had closed up and almost cured.... What is next to be done

to...quiet you, to persuade you to your own interest before your disorders spoil you and devour the country? You cannot imagine what is made by all sorts, and especially those at the helm, of your division. O Friends, I come to you in love. I left you in love, and with resolutions of returning to you.... I am a man of sorrows and you augment my griefs, not because you don't love me, but because you don't love one another.... Cannot you bear a little for the good of the whole, at least till it please God to bring me among you?...Remember your Governor, your friend, and your affectionate one, too, asks this at your hands.

William had more to worry about than just false accusations and squabbling residents in his colony. Because he was now an outlaw, the Crown confiscated all the land in Ireland he had inherited from his father. And he began to wonder whether King William would let him keep Pennsylvania. He held to the hope that because Lord Baltimore was a Catholic and King William hated him more than he hated William, he might get to keep his colony.

The longer William stayed in hiding, the more worried he became. Guli brought him letters from the colony, and every letter contained news of more arguing and strife. Since his cousin William Markham was presently in England, William appointed a new deputy governor. And since he could not find a Quaker who wanted the thankless task, he chose John Blackwell, a former captain in Oliver Cromwell's army.

The new king and queen of England had been right to worry about a plot to bring King James II back to power, but William Penn was not involved in it. In March 1689 James II landed in Kinsale, County Cork, Ireland, with a small army of French and Irish troops. His plan, it seemed, was to march through Catholic Ireland, take a ship to Scotland, and invade England from there.

King William of Orange sent off his first battalion of troops to Ireland in August 1689. King William's War had begun, and William Penn waited in hiding as news of the campaign filtered back to him.

Chapter 14

Losses and Gains

King William and Queen Mary became distracted by the war in Ireland, and William Penn was removed from the list of those wanted for treason. Going home to Guli and the children should have been a happy time for William, but it was not. On November 20, 1689, their youngest child, daughter Guli, died after a short illness. She was four years old and had hardly seen her father during the last year of her life.

Tears streamed down William's face as he watched his daughter's coffin lowered into the ground beside the other Penn children's graves at the Jordans, a Quaker cemetery. As he stood at the graveside, William determined to leave England as soon as he could, he hoped within a year, and take his wife and the remaining three children with him. There was a good home waiting for them at Pennsbury, and his colony needed his firm guidance more than ever.

Leaving was no simple task, however. As the war against King James II raged on in Ireland, it seemed to make the king and queen angrier by the day. Finally, on July 14, 1690, just two weeks after the Battle of the Boyne, Queen Mary signed a royal proclamation ordering the arrest of a number of Catholic sympathizers. Among the names on her list was William Penn. This time William did not hide. He turned himself in.

Once again William found himself staring at the stone walls of the Tower of London, but he did not stay there long. On August 15 he was released on bail, and a hearing of his case was set for November. William had three months to figure out how to protect Pennsylvania in the event he was convicted of being a Catholic sympathizer and sentenced to be beheaded. He was relieved to have Philip Ford, his loyal friend and business adviser, at his side to help plan the next step. In the drawing room at William's Worminghurst home, the two men discussed the problem.

"You have your share of enemies," Philip said.

William nodded in agreement. "I just don't know what to do."

"I have an idea," Philip ventured, "one that would work well if you are willing to trust me completely."

William smiled. "What do you mean *if?* Of course I trust you! Haven't you been handling my accounting since we went to Ireland together?"

"That I have," Philip agreed. "So let me tell you how we can make Pennsylvania secure. I've discussed it already with Bridget, but apart from my wife, no one ever need hear of this."

"What is it you propose?" William asked.

"Owing to the great strife you are in, I think it would be wise for you to protect your colony and your family by signing everything over to me, free and clear. That way if you are convicted they could not take your land from you because it no longer belongs to you, and if you are set free, then we'll forget you ever signed it over. Pennsylvania will remain in your hands."

"I'm not sure. That's a huge decision," William countered.

"But think of it. That way, if you are convicted, I could take care of your family after you are gone. How else can you protect them?"

"Let me think about it," William said.

And he did think about it until on September 3, William Penn agreed to secretly sign papers handing everything he owned over to his trusted Quaker friend. Philip had looked after William's finances for so many years that William felt sure he was doing the best thing for his colony and his family. As time passed, however, he would discover that he had just made a fatal error in judgment.

As it turned out, William need not have worried about his trial. It was played down for political reasons, and he was cleared of all charges against him. He could not breathe easy, however, in the never-ending cat-and-mouse game between him and the royal court. It was only three months later, in February 1691, that Queen Mary issued a new arrest warrant for him. This time William did not turn himself over to the authorities but instead went into hiding. He soon found himself in a sort of legal no-man's-land. The queen had no evidence against him for a trial, but she personally believed that William was plotting against her. Her solution was to keep in place the warrant for his arrest, but she instructed her soldiers not to look for him. That way William could move around the edges of society but not show his head anywhere important for fear of being arrested.

William went into hiding, living with Quaker friends in the poor tenement areas of London where he had gone after his family disowned him for becoming a Quaker twenty-three years before. This time conditions there were worse than ever because of a massive influx of desperately poor people from the country. A new law allowed lords to enclose the public land in their villages, thus cutting common-ers off from access to the land where they grazed their sheep and grew their crops. With no food and no land to grow any on, the people drifted into London's tenements, where unbeknownst to them they lived alongside the governor of Pennsylvania.

Once again William used his time in hiding to write about what he knew. He wrote essays entitled *Some Fruits of Solitude* and *Reflections and Maxims Relating to the Conduct of Human Life*.

On October 13, 1691, royal troops won King William's War in Ireland, and James II retreated to France to live out his remaining days.

A year later William was still officially a wanted man when he got word that the king had ordered the governor of New York, Benjamin Fletcher, to take over Pennsylvania in the name of the Crown. King William did this not to punish William by taking away his land but because French forces were moving down the St. Lawrence River Valley into the Great Lakes. For the British colonies to rebuff them, they would have to band together and form an army. Pennsylvania, with its pacifist views, refused to cooperate, and so Governor Fletcher was told to take the colony over.

William was devastated. It seemed that everything he had worked so hard to achieve and given up so much of his personal freedom for was lost. His Holy Experiment was over, swallowed up by the need to defend the colony from an invading force.

Soon after this devastating news, William received some good news, though he hardly had the heart to rejoice. Many important people had pleaded for the case against him to be dropped, and eventually the king agreed. The secretary of state issued a statement clearing William Penn of all charges, and once again William was a free man.

William hurried home to Worminghurst. Many things had changed in the time he had been in hiding. One of the most obvious changes was the state of his wife's health. Guli looked thin and drawn, weighed down by years of caring for the children alone and worrying about her husband's safety.

William saw little point in going back to Pennsylvania now. Besides, Guli was not well enough to travel, so William once again settled down to life in the Sussex countryside. He spent most of his time at home getting to know the children yet again and reading to Guli. Sometimes he imagined the color was returning to her cheeks, but it was not. On February 23, 1694, Guli called William to her side. He held her hand and prayed with her, and soon afterward she died.

The body of Gulielma Penn was laid to rest in the Jordans graveyard. After the funeral William felt more alone than he ever had before. Guli had stood beside him through all of his trials, raising the children in his absence and never complaining when his standing up for principle cost her as much as or more than it cost him. Now she was gone, and he was alone with three children to raise and little money to keep them.

Nineteen-year-old Springett, though, was a great comfort to William in the days following the funeral. He looked like his mother and had her temperament. He was kind and thoughtful, unlike William Jr., who didn't appear to notice other people's feelings nearly as much.

Despite William's feelings of loss at his wife's death, he had little time to grieve for her, because the king and queen wanted to negotiate a return of Pennsylvania to him. Conditions were attached, and William spent many hours negotiating over them with royal representatives. In December 1694, while William was still negotiating over the conditions for the return of Pennsylvania, Queen Mary died of smallpox, leaving no heir to the throne. The country mourned her passing.

Eventually an agreement was reached, and King William, now the sole monarch of England, agreed that William Penn could have his colony back as long as he promised to provide a militia of eighty men to help defend its borders from the French. If he preferred, instead of hiring men from his colony for the task, he could set aside enough money to pay mercenaries to do the job. This was not something William agreed to easily, since he was committed to the Quaker way of nonviolence, but he had little choice. If he did not provide defense for his colony and indirectly to the colonies around him, Pennsylvania would remain under the direct rule of the Crown. Choosing what in his mind was the lesser of two evils, he agreed to provide a militia. He also agreed to the condition that he return to Pennsylvania and govern it himself. And in returning Pennsylvania, the king finally settled the boundary dispute with Maryland in William's favor.

At the same time Pennsylvania was being returned, King William decided to restore the Penn family land holdings in Ireland to William. William was grateful for their return, especially because it meant that he could once again begin collecting the rent from the tenant farmers who lived on the land.

The thought of returning to Pennsylvania without Guli at his side was a lonely prospect for William. As he thought about it over the next few weeks, a plan formed in his mind. He would not go back to Pennsylvania alone. He would find a new wife to go with him. Of course, this was easier said than done. William was now fifty, and all the years of hiding and uncertainty made him look older than that. His back was stooped, and since Guli's death, his eyes had lost much of their sparkle. Still, he was determined. Whenever he attended a Quaker meeting, he watched out for a suitable wife. Eventually he settled on a thirty-year-old woman named Hannah Callowhill. Hannah had never been married and at her age could not expect to be, except to a widower. William thought she would make an efficient wife and a good companion, though he had no illusions that she would ever replace Guli, who had been the bride of his youth.

The two were married in Hannah's hometown of Bristol on March 5, 1696. William's three children attended the wedding, which was held in Hannah's parents' home. William had wondered whether Springett should come at all, as he appeared to be suffering from a bad case of influenza.

William was so concerned for his eldest son's health that instead of taking a honeymoon he returned to Worminghurst, where the very practical Hannah Penn set straight to work looking after her new stepson. No matter what herbs and remedies she tried, Springett's condition did not improve. In fact, it got worse, until a month after the wedding the Penn family found themselves gathered for Springett's funeral.

It was a somber day, and William grieved the loss of his favorite son. He poured out his feelings in his diary. "So ended the life of my dear child and eldest son...in whom I lost all that any father can lose in a child, since he was capable of anything that became a sober young man; my friend and companion, as well as a most affectionate and dutiful child."

Of William and Guli's eight children, only William Jr. and Letitia remained. Hannah comforted her new husband, and William found that he had married a kind and devoted woman. He was now eager to leave England and begin a new life in his colony. He still had a lot of negotiating to do with the king on behalf of Pennsylvania, and he also needed to set his Irish estates in order now that they had been returned. He was not sure how well they were being managed in the wake of King William's War.

William had another wedding to attend. On January 12, 1699, eighteen-year-old William Jr. married Mary Jones, the twenty-two-year-old daughter of a Bristol merchant. William hoped the young couple would be happy, though he had his doubts. William Jr. had been wild since Springett's death, and William hoped the responsibilities of being a husband would help his son to settle down.

Finally, after the wedding and the settling of all the details relating to Pennsylvania and his Irish estate, William and Hannah set to work supervising the packing of their belongings. They intended to live the rest of their days in Pennsylvania. Twenty-one-year-old Letitia was going with them, but William Jr. and his new bride decided to stay behind at Worminghurst.

As William stepped aboard the sturdy three-masted schooner *Canterbury* on September 3, 1699, his heart was filled with conflicting emotions. On the one hand he was happy to be returning to Pennsylvania. He had been away for sixteen years, much longer than he had ever planned to be gone. But William was also sad. On the voyage back to England sixteen years before, he had looked forward to bringing Guli and the children back to Pennsbury with him. He recalled the excitement of planning the additions to the house there and telling Springett about the stable where he could keep his own horse. Now everything was different. Guli and Springett were buried side-by-side at the Jordans graveyard, and William had a new wife. Still, as if to temper his sadness, Hannah was expecting a baby. The child was due in February, and if it survived, it would be the first Penn born in Pennsylvania.

Chapter 15

The Hand of English Politics

If the wind and the weather cooperated, a ship could make it across the Atlantic Ocean in under two months, but the passengers aboard the *Canterbury* had no such luck. The ship was pushed off course by strong winds, and no navigational equipment in 1699 was capable of telling the captain of a ship his exact location at sea. By the time the Capes of Delaware were sighted, the ship had been at sea for twelve weeks. Indeed, many people waiting for the ship to arrive in Pennsylvania presumed it had been lost at sea. Other ships that left after the *Canterbury* had made it to the colony with news that William and Hannah Penn were aboard the ship. So when the *Canterbury* was finally sighted making its way into Delaware Bay, everyone breathed a sigh of relief.

The ship headed up the Delaware River, past New Castle, where William had first set foot in America, to Chester, the new name given to Upland. As the *Canterbury* dropped anchor, the citizens of the town streamed out to catch a glimpse of their legendary leader.

It was at Chester, in December 1699, that William Penn again set foot on his beloved land. Hundreds of people cheered and welcomed their governor ashore. William had dressed for the occasion in his finest red silk suit with gold braiding.

A cannon boomed a welcome for William, once, twice, and then a third time. Then a scream pierced the celebration. "Get the doctor!" someone yelled from the crowd.

William watched as the ship's surgeon grabbed his bag of tools and plunged into the crowd.

"What's happening?" William asked.

"It's the lad who shot the cannon, Governor," replied one of the dignitaries standing beside William. "They say he put the third plug of powder into the barrel before the sponger had time to clean it out. It exploded and shot his arm to pieces."

"Clear more space. I need to amputate. Someone get me brandy!" yelled the surgeon.

The crowd grew quiet, and then a minute or two later came more screams. "Fire! Fire!" was the cry.

Some of the brandy that was used to sedate the young victim had spilled onto the surgeon's apron and had been accidentally ignited by a person holding a welcome torch.

"Get him on the ground! Douse him with water!" William heard someone else say.

Soon the fire was out, and the surgeon completed the task of cutting the young man's arm off before he retired to his cabin to sooth his burns with butter.

Once the commotion had died down, the welcome ceremony continued.

That night after the festivities ended, William and Hannah returned to the *Canterbury*, and the following morning the ship sailed upriver to Philadelphia.

"I am anxious to see the city again," William told his wife as they passed the confluence with the Schuylkill River. "When I left sixteen years ago Philadelphia was still under construction. I am told there are over seven hundred homes there now, each one with a lawn around it as I imagined. I can hardly wait to walk the streets Thomas Holme and I laid out together!"

Soon that is just what William was doing. Even though he had received letters updating him on Philadelphia's growth, it was still a thrill to see for himself what had happened in the intervening years. The city was so unlike any in Europe, with its wide streets, sturdy brick houses, and abundant trees. The docks bustled with activity as a procession of ships unloaded every conceivable item the people of the colony would need and then returned to England with the products of Pennsylvania: lumber, furs, tobacco, potash, hemp, linen, whale oil, copper, and iron.

As William walked around, escorted by the lieutenant governor, he was just as pleased to see the
smiling faces of so many different people. There
were many Quakers, of course. They made up
about half the population of the colony, but there
were many others too. Moravians, Lutherans,
Catholics, and Jews had come to Pennsylvania to
live their lives in an atmosphere of peace and religious freedom. Indians, too, walked freely along
the streets. And that was exactly the way William
Penn wanted it. Pennsylvania was not a Quaker
colony, but a colony based upon the Quaker principles of tolerance for others and religious liberty
and justice for all its citizens. Anyone who needed
refuge from the terror of persecution could find a
home in Pennsylvania. That fact alone made all of
the difficulties and expenses William had endured
over the past years worthwhile.

Of course William still had many problems to
attend to. After all, he had been away from the
colony for sixteen years. He moved his family into a
house in Philadelphia until the baby was born and
plunged himself into the work with an enthusiasm
he hadn't felt since Guli's death.

At the end of January 1700 there was news of
two births in the Penn family. Hannah had given
birth to a son, whom they named John and whom
William referred to as "The Little American." Word
also arrived from Worminghurst in England that
William Jr. and Mary had had a baby girl, whom
they named Gulielma. William couldn't have been
happier.

After the birth of John, William moved his family the twenty-four miles upriver to Pennsbury. What a wonderful sight the estate was, nestled beside the river. All the work William had ordered done to the place during the years he was away was complete. Pennsbury looked every bit the grand estate William had imagined it would be. Around the house were beds of roses that William's gardener had brought from England, and the walnut trees William had imagined on his first trip were now a reality. The trees stood in rows with their boughs stretched wide. Rows of fruit trees—apples, pears, plums, peaches, cherries, quince, even some apricot and fig trees—adorned the property.

After the family was settled into their new home, William began to inspect the Quaker schools in Pennsylvania. He liked what he saw, but he was concerned that it was mainly Quaker children who were getting an education. He had a vision for all children receiving a free, public education, and so he ordered that the Quaker schools accept all children, even girls and Indians. Every child in the colony had to attend school until he or she turned twelve.

This decision made some people in the colony angry. Farmers asked who would help with the harvest if their children were made to go to school. But William stood his ground. He believed that Pennsylvania was to be an example, a light to the other colonies that all citizens should be able to read and write and understand how their government works.

Unlike most other early American colonists, William Penn had the peculiar idea that the colonies should be joined to one another instead of each being joined individually to England. As a result, he set the date of October 1, 1700, for a conference and invited the governors of New York, Massachusetts, and Virginia to join him in New York to discuss the idea of a union of American colonies.

Governor Blackistone of Massachusetts sent word that he was too sick to attend, but the earl of Bellomont, the governor of New York, and Colonel Nicholson, the governor of Virginia, arrived as planned. At first they were skeptical about the notion until William, using all his legal skills, laid out the reasons why a union would be a good idea. He explained that the united colonies could all use one currency, making trade among them easier. A mint could be set up in New York so that they would not have to wait for money to come from England. Sometimes coins were in such short supply that merchants had to revert to a bartering system. William also pointed out that the united colonies would all be safer places. Criminals could not cross into another colony to escape punishment for their crimes, and the colonies could work together to defeat pirates and keep the waterways open to trading ships.

Gradually the other governors understood the genius of what William was proposing, and at the end of four days they signed a report outlining their ideas about working together and sent it to the Lords of Trade in London. Before the document was dispatched, Governor Blackistone also signed it.

What none of the governors knew, however, was that by the time their report arrived in England, Parliament had much more pressing matters to deal with. On November 1, 1700, King Charles II of Spain died, creating an opportunity for Spain and France to be united under the French King Louis XIV. King William and the British Parliament were very worried about this possibility. Once again it would make the Catholic countries far too powerful, so England prepared for war.

When he read about this new development, William desperately wished that the American colonies could distance themselves from the looming troubles of Europe. However, the colonies were flanked by French territories to the north and west and by the Spanish to the south. If war broke out in Europe, it would surely cast its ugly shadow over America as well.

As the months went by, the news was even worse than William had expected. Parliament appeared to want control over all the colonies in America so it could raise troops from them and direct their efforts should a war break out. Most of the other colonies, including Maryland, were now Crown colonies, with a royal governor appointed from London to rule them. William Penn had a sick feeling that Parliament was planning to end his proprietorship of Pennsylvania and make it into another Crown colony.

In August 1701 William wrote to a friend in England, "I only wish myself twenty years younger and no Englishman. I would hope to enjoy the fruit of my labor and receive the return of my deep and sinking experience." He wanted to be let alone to run his colony, but it was not to be. Soon William learned that a bill was to be brought before Parliament to strip him of his colony. At the same time, he learned that England had formed the Grand Alliance with the League of Augsburg, Denmark, Portugal, and Holland to fight the French. War, it seemed, was inevitable.

William sat up all night trying to think of some way to avoid returning to England to plead for the right to keep proprietorship of Pennsylvania. But as the dawn broke, he knew he had once again been defeated by European politics. His only hope was to go to London and appear before Parliament himself.

"If you are going, I am coming with you!" Hannah told her husband when he broke the news to her.

"But, Hannah, my dear," William reasoned, "I will be gone only six months at the most. It seems such an inconvenience to you and little John, and besides, you have another baby on the way. It's not a wise idea. And someone will need to stay with Letitia."

Hannah laughed. "I'm sure Letitia will leap at the chance to return to England. Haven't you noticed how bored she is here? Besides, she wants to visit her Aunt Margaret and see young William's children."

"But we have a home here," William countered, although he sensed nothing was going to stand in Hannah's way.

"And we have a home in England, too. If the trip is short, we shan't be gone long. And if it takes you more time than you thought, well then, I would not want to be separated from you for a long period."

William thought about what Hannah said. Maybe she was right. Maybe they should stay together. No one had any idea where the Grand Alliance might lead. The French could attack England or Pennsylvania.

Shortly before William left for England, a group of Indians gathered at Pennsbury to bid him farewell and reaffirm the covenant of friendship they had made with him and the people of Pennsylvania. Many of those who came had been present seventeen years before at the meeting under the elm tree in Shackamaxon, where the covenant of friendship between the Indians and William had been established. The Indians remembered William fondly from his first stay in Pennsylvania. They were genuinely glad to see him when he returned to the colony, and now they were concerned about how long he would be gone. Still, as they had done before, in William's absence they would abide by the covenant they had made with him.

Before William left, six Indian chiefs dictated a letter to King William and Parliament reminding them of what a good man William Penn was.

We the Kings and Sachems of the Ancient Nations of the Susquehannah and Shavanah Indians, understanding that our Loving and good friend Brother William Penn is to our great grief and the trouble of all the Indians of these parts obliged to go back to England...acknowledge that he has been not only just but always very kind to us...not suffering us to receive any wrong from any of the people under his government. Giving us, as is well known, his house for our home at all times, and freely entertaining us at his own cost, and often filling us with many presents of necessary goods for our clothing and other accommodations.
Besides that he had paid us for our lands, which no Governor ever did before him, and we hope that the Great King of the English will be good and kind to him and his children. Then we shall have confidence that we and our children and people will be well used and be encouraged to live among the Christians according to the agreement that he and we have solemnly made, for as long as the Sun and the Moon shall endure, One head, one mouth and one heart.
We could say much of his good council and instructions, which he has often given

us and our people, to live a sober and virtuous life as the best way to please the great God and be happy here and forever. But let this suffice to the great King and his wise sachems in love to our good friend and brother William Penn.

Tears came to William's eyes as he read their letter. He noted on the back of it "The Indian Kings' Address to the King and Parliament" and packed it into his leather pouch for the trip back to England.

On November 3, 1701, William, Hannah, John "The Little American," and Letitia boarded the *Dolmahoy* for a winter crossing of the Atlantic Ocean. As they sailed away, William stood on deck and watched the coastline of America dip below the horizon. He counted up the time he had spent in Pennsylvania with his family—twenty-two months. He had come to Pennsylvania to stay for good, and now after less than two years, the hand of English politics had once again reached out across the ocean and taken him from his beloved Holy Experiment.

Chapter 16

Burdened Down

O n January 4, 1702, William Penn picked up a quill and addressed a letter to James Logan, his friend and representative in Philadelphia, to let him know the family had arrived safely in England. He began, "We had a swift passage—twenty-six days from the capes to soundings, and thirty to Portsmouth, with five of the last days clear for observation, before we came to the channel. The captain very civil and all the company. Tishe [Letitia] and Johnne [John], after the first five days, hearty and well, and Johnne exceeding cheerful all the way."

William then sat for a long time trying to decide what he should write next. He knew that James Logan wanted to know how William Jr. was behaving, mainly because he was in line to be the next proprietor of Pennsylvania. Yet William dared not

tell anyone the whole truth. His son was a drunk-
ard and a gambler who hardly took care of his wife
or the two children he now had. William's only hope
was that his presence would help the twenty-two-
year-old to grow up at last and make something of
all the opportunities he had. In the end, William
wrote, "I find Billie very serviceable, but costly."

William stared for a long time at what he had
written. Costly was an understatement! While
William had been away, William Jr. had racked up
huge gambling and drinking debts, which he
expected his father to bail him out of. William pondered why things had gone so wrong for the only
surviving son from his first marriage. Was it
because his mother died when he was fourteen
and his older brother, Springett, two years later?
Was it because he had been away from home for
such long periods when William Jr. was young? He
didn't know, nor did he know what to do with his
son now, except to try to interest him in Pennsylvania and hope he mended his ways.

Although William worried about his son,
another worry was lifted from his shoulders, at
least for the time being. Parliament had indeed
introduced a bill to strip William Penn of his proprietorship of Pennsylvania and make it a royal
colony. However, the bill had been quashed, and it
was unlikely that another bill would be introduced
in the foreseeable future, since it seemed that
England might go to war with France.

Worry about the future of his colony, however,
soon came bearing down again on William, this
time from an unexpected quarter. In January

1702, very soon after William's return to England, his financial manager and fellow Quaker, Philip Ford, died suddenly. William attended his funeral and paid respects to his wife, Bridget, son Philip Jr., and two daughters. He was surprised when two days later Bridget showed up at the house where he was staying in London.

"See what I've got here, Mr. Penn!" Bridget said, waving a piece of paper in front of his face.

"My dear lady, please sit down and compose yourself. Do you need my help with something?" William inquired.

"Ha! You help me?" she snarled. "When I've finished what I have to say, you will find it's you who will be begging for my help. Here, let me read this to you. It's my dear husband's will, you know." She spread the document gleefully on the table in front of her and began to read. "As the sole owner of the properties formerly owned by William Penn, in the Colony of Pennsylvania, I hereby do order those properties to be sold upon my death, with my wife and children as beneficiaries, unless William Penn wishes to buy them back within six months' time, for the sum of eleven thousand pounds."

William was stunned. He tried to piece together what he had just heard.

"And in case you are wondering," Bridget went on viciously, "my lawyer has the papers in which you signed over all of your holdings in Pennsylvania to my husband."

Slowly William understood the terrible deed his trusted friend had done. Instead of ripping up the papers William had signed before his trial for treason, Philip had kept them, and now in his will he was using them to claim that he owned all of Pennsylvania! William felt the color drain from his face. His voice shook as he spoke. "I think you had better leave now, Mrs. Ford. If you could leave a copy of the will, I would be grateful. I will call on you as soon as I can."

"But what do you say?" Bridget pressed. "Rumor has it that you don't have the money to pay! Is that right?"

William stood up and guided her to the door. "I cannot say more now, Madame. You must leave me in peace."

Once she had gone and the door was closed, William locked it, sat down in a leather chair by the fire, put his face in his hands, and wept. He wept bitterly over the possibility of losing his colony to Bridget Ford, and he wept for the legal battles that he knew surely lay ahead. But most of all he wept over Philip Ford. Philip had been William's trusted friend and employee for over thirty-seven years, and more than that, he had been a fellow Quaker. How could he have done such an awful thing? It was almost too much to bear.

William knew he needed help to sort through the situation. He invited Henry Gouldney and Guli's uncle, Herbert Springett, to read through all his personal paperwork. What they found saddened William even more, though by now he was beyond the point of shock. It was clear that Philip had been swindling William for many years. William had always trusted his business manager's description of what he was signing, but now he was finding out that what he thought he had signed and what he actually signed were very different!

At every turn Philip had used William's business dealings to squeeze money out of him. He charged William interest rates higher than were legally allowed. He had also paid himself outrageously large commissions from William's money for business he had done on behalf of the Pennsylvania colony. As well, a number of the accounting books were mysteriously missing.

Henry Gouldney and Herbert Springett both felt that William probably had a good chance of proving that Philip Ford had been dishonest for many years and swindled him out of a lot more than the eleven thousand pounds he was now supposed to pay to get Pennsylvania back.

Meanwhile, Bridget Ford and her children refused to allow a group of Quaker men to settle the dispute, which was the way William wanted the situation resolved. William found it distressing to think that everyone would hear how one Quaker had taken advantage of another. Bridget insisted that the case be heard in a Crown courtroom, and William began preparing for a trial.

On March 8, 1702, while out riding, King William fell from his horse, banged his head hard on the ground, and died. Thankfully, he had already named the Protestant Princess Anne Stuart, his dead wife Mary's younger sister, as his successor to the throne. Queen Anne quickly took over the royal affairs.

The day after the king's death, Hannah gave birth to another baby, another son. They named him Thomas after Hannah's father.

While the arrival of a new son should have been a happy time for William, it wasn't. The baby's birth combined with the king's death to weigh on William's heart even more. With King William gone, no one knew if Queen Anne would declare war on France, which would in turn plunge the colonies into war. And with the arrival of a new son, William was reminded that he had to get money from somewhere to support his growing family while he stayed in England.

Nothing was more frustrating than trying to collect the money for the taxes he was owed in Pennsylvania. It wasn't all the colonists' fault. There simply was not enough money in the colonies for them to run efficiently. Parliament forbade the colonies from minting their own money, and so the colonies used gold and silver coins from other countries, mainly Holland, France, and Portugal. Because it wasn't always easy to get ahold of foreign money, people either used the wampum shell necklaces that the Indians used or bartered their goods. William and James Logan corresponded and decided that the best answer to the situation was for the colonists to pay their quitrents in the form of produce such as flour, pork, tobacco, beaver pelts, and beer, all of which could be shipped to London. It wasn't an ideal solution, as it left William with the job of selling the produce when it arrived, but it allowed him to make some money from his colony.

Queen Anne and the English Parliament, along with the Grand Alliance, declared war on France on May 4, 1702. In England it was called the War of the Spanish Succession, while in the colonies it became known as Queen Anne's War. The name the war went by did not matter to William. What mattered was that the war endangered his colony and made his already faltering financial situation even more precarious. Now the ships bringing produce across the Atlantic Ocean for William were often captured by French privateers, or dishonest captains plundered the cargo themselves and then blamed it on the French. The whole matter of collecting quitrents became a bigger nightmare than William could have imagined.

In the midst of all this turmoil, Letitia made known her intention to marry a London merchant named William Aubrey. Now William had a large dowry to worry about paying as well. And to make matters worse, Bridget Ford paid William another visit. This time she had an even grander idea. She told William that according to the lawyer the papers in her possession conferred on her the right to the governorship of Pennsylvania! William recoiled at the thought of Governor Bridget Ford, and as soon as she left, he went straight to talk to Henry Gouldney and Herbert Springett about the matter.

On August 20, 1702, Letitia and William Aubrey were married. It was a bright spot in an otherwise depressing period in William Penn's life.

William Jr. and his wife produced another son around this time and named the baby William. But even the arrival of another child didn't seem to deter William Jr. from his extravagant ways.

More than anything else, William Penn wanted to return to Pennsylvania, but that was not possible.

The following year, on July 30, 1703, William and Hannah's third child, a daughter whom they named Hannah Margarita, was born in Bristol. Again, the arrival of another child should have been a happy time for William, but it was not. In fact, his pressing legal problems kept him in London, and it was several months before he even got to see his new daughter. Weighed down by so many concerns, William longed for Pennsylvania. But he had to face the fact that he would not be returning to his colony for a long time. Bridget Ford had him tied down with legal suits that would take years to sort out.

William had little choice but to send his son William Jr. to Pennsylvania as his representative. He knew it was a risk sending someone who had not proved himself to be responsible, but he hoped that getting his son away from his gambling friends and giving him an important task would wake him up to the realities of life. On December 3, William Penn, Jr. set sail for America. He traveled alone, leaving his wife and three children behind at Worminghurst for his father to support.

About this time word reached London that local Indians who sided with the French had attacked settlements in Maine. Just as William had predicted, the war in Europe was spilling over onto American soil. Everyone was anxious to find out

what the Indians would do next. William waited to
hear any news that came from Pennsylvania. He
also waited to hear news of how his son was doing.

The first few letters from members of the council
in the colony were encouraging, but slowly William
detected a sour note creeping into the correspon-
dence. Finally, nearly a year later, William heard a
rumor that his son had been in a street brawl with
a night watchman. William hoped it was not true,
but a letter soon arrived confirming that the rumor
was indeed true and pointing out that his son was
now known in the colony by the nickname "William
the Waster." William Penn was horrified. Quakers
stood for hard work and simple living—values that
his son evidently did not possess!

William wrote to James Logan asking him to
send his son straight home to England. It was an
ironic reversal from the time when William's own
father had sent for him to come home from Ireland
so many years before. In that case Sir William
Penn was worried that his son was too concerned
about religious matters and not interested enough
in worldly affairs. Now William Jr. was coming
home to face a father who thought him too interested in the world and not concerned enough with
his own soul.

The situation broke William's heart, and William
began questioning whether starting a colony had
been worth the cost of a wayward son. He finished
his letter to James Logan with the words, "O
Pennsylvania! what hast thou cost me? Above thirty
thousand pounds more than I ever got by it, two

hazardous and most fatiguing voyages, my straits and slavery here, and my child's soul almost...."

Indeed, so burdened down with cares was William Penn that he began to think about a different solution to his problems over Pennsylvania. He desperately wanted to avoid Bridget Ford's getting her hands on the place, and the colony had become a source of financial strain and heartache. A solid framework of laws that embodied William's principles of liberty, justice, and religious tolerance for every individual was now in place in the colony. That was what mattered most to William, not the proprietorship of the colony. So William petitioned the Lords of Trade, whose job it was to oversee the colonies, to take Pennsylvania off his hands. He would surrender control of his colony to the Crown for a cash settlement and "some few privileges that will not be thought...unreasonable."

The government was immediately interested in William's offer, but it balked at some of his privileges. In particular, it did not like the condition William laid down that the government agree to uphold the laws of Pennsylvania and the civil liberties granted the colony's residents. The government, while eager to get its hands on Pennsylvania, thought that in return for a cash payment William Penn should surrender his colony "unconditionally." But the laws and civil liberties of Pennsylvania were the ideals William had fought all his life to see established. William would not compromise, though he continued to negotiate with the government.

As the matter of the possibility of selling Pennsylvania back to the government dragged on, Hannah produced three more children, Margaret, Richard, and Dennis, bringing the total number of children she and William had to six, and they were all under eight years of age! William loved his second family, though at sixty-two he did find their constant activity a little wearing during the long English winters.

On May 17, 1707, William received some bad news. He knew that Philip Ford had been swindling him for many years, and he had the account books now to prove it. However, there were so many account books, deeds, and land titles that it had taken William years to sort the whole matter out. Upon looking at all of the paperwork involved with the case, the Lord Chancellor declared it too complicated and ordered that William's case could be based only upon land deeds. No other paperwork was to be admitted into evidence. This decision was a great blow to William, mainly because he had signed land deeds over to Philip at various times, in some cases without knowing what he had signed, and in other cases on a "gentleman's agreement" that the documents would never be presented.

Now, sensing that victory would soon be hers, Bridget Ford became even more vicious. She filed a new lawsuit against William claiming that he owed her back rent on all of the property she held the deeds to. This suit, which was much less complicated, quickly worked its way through the court system. William lost the case and was left with two choices: either hand over the back rent plus interest or flee the country.

William's sense of justice had not left him. He would not accept the court's decision, because the court had not been willing to review all of the paperwork in the case, nor would he run away and hide. Instead the sixty-three-year-old Quaker governor of Pennsylvania decided he would hold his head up and continue about his business.

On January 7, 1708, William attended a Quaker meeting in Gracechurch Street, where he had been arrested years before for allegedly starting a riot. Everyone sat quietly in meditation in the meeting hall when two bailiffs sent by Bridget Ford burst in. William stood up, but the two men on either side of him told him to remain where he was. They walked over and talked to the bailiffs. Several minutes later the bailiffs left, and the Quakers returned to their seats.

"They came to arrest you," one of them said, "but we told them there was no need to disrupt the meeting, and that you would surrender yourself to them when the service was over."

That night William Penn found himself once more in jail. This time, however, it was not the Tower of London, but the Fleet, London's debtor's prison. As William sat in prison, he had little idea of the commotion that was swirling outside. Not only his Quaker friends but also many others were incensed that Bridget Ford would be so disrespectful as to have William Penn arrested in the middle of a religious meeting.

Several influential Quakers asked to look over the accounting books that Philip Ford had kept. Within a month or so, everyone agreed that William Penn had been the victim of a greedy and ruthless plot. William was released from the Fleet and put under house arrest. No sooner had he settled himself into a small house nearby than he received word that his four-year-old daughter Hannah had died after a short illness.

William was upset that he could not go to Bristol to be with his wife, who was too distraught to travel to him. He waited anxiously for word of the funeral, and it was not until May that Hannah returned to her husband's side. She left their five children, John, Thomas, Margaret, Richard, and Dennis, in Bristol with her parents.

William was still under house arrest when Hannah had another baby in September. It was a girl, whom they named Hannah in honor of the big sister she would never know.

A week after baby Hannah's birth, William received the news he had waited so long to hear. The case brought against him by Bridget Ford was over. He was allowed to retain ownership of Pennsylvania, though the court ordered him to pay seven thousand six hundred pounds to Philip Ford's estate to clear all debts involved in the case.

Although William did not have the cash to pay that amount, several of his Quaker friends stepped forward to loan the money to him. Finally the case was settled. The weight that had burdened William for six long years had been lifted from his shoulders. William determined to return to Pennsylvania one more time, and this time, he promised himself, he would never again leave.

Chapter 17

The Greatest Lawgiver

There was to be no speedy return to Pennsylvania. William was still negotiating with the government about surrendering control of his colony to the Crown. Negotiations had been dragging on for several years, and still no agreement had been reached.

Soon after the legal battle with Bridget Ford was settled, more tragedy struck the Penn family. Four-month-old Hannah followed her namesake to the grave. She was buried at the Jordans graveyard, where six of William's other children already lay. Indeed, William worried about the other children, especially in winter, when many children died from influenza. He wrote to his nine-year-old son John "The American," who was staying with his grandparents in Bristol.

Take care of thy little horse daily and don't ride alone, nor in the dirt without thy sashoons [leather leg padding] to fill the feet of the boot, to keep thee dry and warm. Remember what I say and I desire both thou and brother Tomme [Thomas] may have as strong and thick shoes as friend Kippen made for Arthur at his coming away, and then you may go in the wet and dirt more safely.

In 1707 William had been forced to sell the family home at Worminghurst to help pay some of his debts, and it was not until May 1710 that the Penn family were living under one roof again. William rented a large country house at Ruscombe, near Twyford in Berkshire. The family, along with their servants, moved in on a cold winter's day. Soon afterward, William Jr., with his wife and three children, also moved into the house, and the bedrooms were shuffled around to make space for them all.

Everyone loved living in the country again, especially the older boys, who were fond of horse riding. William liked the place, too. He had always preferred country living to the crowded city, but most of all, he longed for the negotiations for the transfer of Pennsylvania to be over so that the family could all return to America.

Finally, in February 1711, the Lords of Trade and the queen agreed on the terms for the surrender of Pennsylvania. William would be paid twelve thousand pounds over a seven-year period for his interest in the colony, and he would retain the right to name the next governor.

A lot of paperwork had to be completed before the agreement could be finalized, and in October 1712, William was still in England eagerly awaiting completion of the paperwork so that he could return to Pennsylvania. On October 4 he sat writing a letter to his old friend James Logan, when suddenly his pen stopped in midsentence and his hand fell from the page. Hannah rushed to his side and helped him to bed. She then called for a doctor, who diagnosed William with lethargic illness. William had suffered a stroke.

Like many stroke victims, William began to recover. Soon he could write and speak again, though he found the hustle and bustle of London too much for him. He preferred staying at Ruscombe, where the pace of life was slower and he could look out across the hedges and wheat fields.

A year later William suffered another stroke. This time he did not recover nearly as well. Hannah had to help him dress, and the children took turns reading to him, since William could no longer focus his eyes on the page. He also loved to go to the local Quaker meeting, but he did not speak much anymore.

Bit by bit, even the little William could do for himself dwindled away, until he completely lost his memory. It was a long, slow good-bye that ended on the night of July 30, 1718, when William Penn, governor of Pennsylvania, died. William was buried beside Guli, his first wife, in the graveyard at the

Jordans, where he had wept and mourned for so many people who had been dear to him over the years.

Because of William's stroke, the paperwork for the transfer of Pennsylvania to the Crown was never completed. The Penn family retained official ownership of Pennsylvania until the time of the Revolutionary War, when all royal charters were dissolved.

In 1751 a bell was hung in the Pennsylvania State House at Philadelphia. The bell celebrated the fiftieth anniversary of the *Charter of Privileges,* the farsighted framework of laws William Penn had put in place in his colony. The bell was inscribed with the words "Proclaim liberty throughout the land unto all the inhabitants thereof." And indeed in 1776, with the signing of the Declaration of Independence, that is what the bell did. The Liberty Bell, as we know it today, rang out to proclaim liberty to all those within its hearing.

While William Penn, in the end, spent only a short period of time in Pennsylvania, in the time he was there he left an indelible mark upon the place. And when a group of men gathered together in his city of Philadelphia in 1787 to draft a constitution for the fledgling United States of America, the ideals of William Penn from nearly a hundred years before about liberty, justice, fairness, and tolerance guided much of their thinking and discussion. Indeed, Thomas Jefferson, one of the men present at that gathering, called William Penn "the greatest lawgiver the world has produced."

Coote, Stephen. *Samuel Pepys: A Life.* Palgrave (St. Martin's Press), 2000.

Dolson, Hildegarde. *William Penn: Quaker Hero.* Random House, 1961.

Dunn, Mary Maples. *William Penn: Politics and Conscience.* Princeton University Press, 1967.

Fantel, Hans. *William Penn: Apostle of Dissent.* William Morrow & Company, 1974.

Peare, Catherine Owens. *William Penn: A Biography.* J. B. Lippincott, 1957.

Remember William Penn. William Penn Tercentenary Committee, 1944.

Syme, Ronald. *William Penn: The Founder of Pennsylvania.* William Morrow & Company, 1966.

Tolles, Frederick B. *Quakers and the Atlantic Culture.* Macmillan, 1960.

Trueblood, D. Elton. *The People Called Quakers.* Harper & Row, 1966.

About the Authors

Janet and Geoff Benge are a husband and wife writing team with over twenty years of writing experience. Janet is a former elementary school teacher. Geoff holds a degree in history. Together they have a passion to make history come alive for a new generation of readers.

Originally from New Zealand, the Benges make their home in the Orlando, Florida, area.

Also from Janet and Geoff Benge...

More adventure-filled biographies for ages 10 to 100!

Unit Study Curriculum Guides are available for select biographies.

Available from YWAM Publishing
1-800-922-2143 / www.ywampublishing.com